CW00407196

INTERVIEW WITH AN ALIEN

BOOK ONE

STEVE & EVAN LEA KAPITELI
STRONG

Publication details

INTERVIEW WITH AN ALIEN
BY STEVE & EVAN STRONG
LEA KAPITELI

© 2022 Printed in Australia.
All characters and events in this book are based on factual people and happenings
from around the world and beyond. Any resemblance of these characters and
events from other media sources is purely coincidental.

This book is protected under the copyright laws of Australia. Any reproduction or
unauthorized use of material or artwork contained within this book is prohibited
without the express permission from the author and/or publication.

The author and/or publication has not authorized any sales of this book without
its cover and/or publication page. If you procured this copy of the book without
a cover, then the author and/or publisher has not received payment for this copy.

Printed and distributed by IngramSpark
https://www.ingramspark.com/

Illustrations by Lea Kapiteli.

Cover design by Erica Schmerbeck & Lea Kapiteli

This edition was initially printed as a paperback cover.

About the Authors

Steve Strong is a secondary school teacher with a background in Archaeology and Education. He was involved in the formation of a Graduate Diploma of Aboriginal Education for the N.S.W. Department of Education, writing units on Traditional Law and Contemporary History. He also co-authored the highly successful "Aboriginal Australia: A Language and Cultural kit".

~

Evan Strong has a background in Anthropology & Indigenous Cultural Studies, Counselling & Mediation with a Bachelor's Degree in Social Sciences and Graduate Studies in Psychology. Evan has worked as a researcher for the Northern Rivers Area Health Service, a Social Worker, Teachers Aide.

~

Lea Kapiteli was born in New Zealand in 1993 into a Croatian family that migrated to Australia in 1998. Aaand more importantly: she has been in psychic contact with extra-terrestrials and extra-dimensionals since early childhood, even recalls some of her past lives and the numbing existence beyond life.

@Forgotten Origins   @StarnovisLea   ouralienancestry.net

Table of Contents

Contents

Foreign Friends
Lea Kapiteli

Section 1 – The Beginning

Alien contact didn't start in the middle 20th century as many would have you believe it. It didn't start when I was a child either. It was long before that; it was so long ago, that 'our' and 'their' history blended. In many respects, I am human now, but I was not before this life. Nor was I an extra-terrestrial. I was just a disembodied soul floating in the aether, wondering and wandering what my next life should be. Just like you, I was a soul, whether you remember it or not.

In the beyond, that's where I see him. He comes forth with an opportunity that I eagerly await to deny. He is wiser and greater than me, but I smirk and scoff. He isn't offended, in fact, there's begging to his tone – a desperation for me to help him. I told him I was done with Earth and Earth was done with me. Atlantis left me with a parting gift: an eternal scar for my immortal soul. I couldn't bare the pain of being human again. He paused.

"I remember Atlantis, too," he said after a while.

"Then how can you ask me to go through that again, Mezreth?" I said.

"Look," he showed me life stretch across the blue world. Plentiful and messy, not unlike what I remember during the Atlantean Empire. When I looked closer, it was different. The humans were not psychic, they couldn't see the soul of the wilds. Oh no, the trees … burning and cutting. Oh no, the valleys breaking open and their insides melted into weapons for war. Oh no, the animals left to die in wasted forests or worse, be forced into tiny cages that would become their whole worlds.

"I have seen enough," I said pulling away, "I'm sorry for what's happening there, but how can you expect me to overcome such atrocities?"

"You won't be alone; there are others who are like you already alive, even when you believe you are singular. You won't be alone; I have been here while you were not, and I shall remain, even when you decide to leave for another life on another world," he said.

"Will you abandon me like before?"

"Not for a single day," he said.

I knew what was coming, for I had fallen into new countless lives and I forgot how many. However, unlike last time – Mezreth would be my eyes in the stars. The weight of life squeezed around my soul and felt the anchor drop down into the dark wet depths of a new womb.

I can't remember when I opened my eyes or when I stood for the first time; I can't remember realising my arms and new body – it was instinctive and natural. I rode the waves of being until the spikes of curiosity roused my consciousness. I do remember fragments of a small, shadowed humanoid standing in the hallway spotlight into my bedroom door as I curled in on my race car bed and gentle whispers of a woman's voice in my ear while I sat among toys who were my only company. There were many more of these moments but were washed from memory.

The first tangible memory of what would be my life-long friends, was suddenly waking in my bedroom. It was night, I knew that. It was supposed to be dark, but it wasn't. A pearly blue light poured through the window and deep inside me, and I had to go – and I did. I didn't stop for the window, as if the glass had ceased to exist. What should have been my backyard, became a walkway to a door, and there, another small figure stood. She barely reached over my height, but I knew she was old. Her dark face held a pair of large, unnerving lime eyes and her gold skin was covered in a slippery red robe. Her round head was bare of hair and her scalp was adorned with sparkling bronze jewellery. She beckoned me through the door.

Later, when I started talking about my experiences, I was asked if I was on a ship, but I wouldn't know. The walls and ceiling in the wide room seemed to be moving and a strange light blanketed all the people within. There were children wearing pyjamas playing with children wearing different clothes – even their faces were strange. There were adults looming in the background, some were smiling, but all were observing. Despite these oddities, they didn't stain the light and joyous air in the glimmering room. My anxieties were akin to any room full of new people at my kindergarten.

The golden lady gave the faintest gesture to a purple lady sitting alone on a short table outside of the circle of playing children. I sat beside her, and she smiled. I remember she was warm, though I cannot remember ever touching her. I saw rainbows around her, though I cannot remember if it was her clothes or an energy my higher senses could perceive.

"My name is Ahntajisan," she introduced herself. She didn't wait or expect me to reply, it was as if she had already known me. She was taller than the golden woman and had violet hair. She looked like a woman, barring the skin and the ethereal glow.

"Play with each toy I give you, and when we are finished, you can play with the others," she said before sliding a pyramid-like shaped object to me. It was black and white, it was slick to the touch, but as I pressed, I realised that there were smaller triangles falling apart in my hand. I pulled at it, piece by piece before reassembling. She said nothing, I almost forgot she was there – and where I was. Her delicate hand slid it out of sight before passing over another teal lump in front of me. It was doughy, but firm, I forced more of my fingers into it. I squeezed a handle and began waving it until the hard dough softened so much that it slimed over my fingers and knuckles.

Piece by piece, toy by toy, Ahntajisan would bring before me and take away. I cannot remember the other toys or when she dismissed me, but the very last memory of that night was sitting by with the other children, playing with a finger-spinning frisbee. We all watched the baby-blue ring levitate above our heads before losing speed, and ultimately, dropping.

The following day and following days were a blur to my young mind. It was school, friends, TV and family as usual, except for unusual pieces of knowledge that crept up on my surface thoughts. I remember telling my mother that we were made by aliens. All of humanity was made by them, I still remember fragments of viewing the endless corridors of bio-engineering bays with tanks lining the walls and alien faces looking at me and smiling. I don't believe that memory was a physical visitation, but something more special.

I was asked by people over the years if I had any negative experiences with these beings, and my answer has always been the same: never. However, it does not mean every experience was pleasant. I saw the golden lady's lime eyes smile at me when she put a strange silvery-white crescent-shaped helmet over my crown. She hesitated for a moment; I felt she was warning me something was going to happen and it might be unpleasant. I was unafraid. Then the humming crept into my mind. It purred louder and louder. I was still unafraid. The purr transformed into a gurgling hum. My body cringed as loudness pained through my ears, but the room was silent.

The golden lady snapped the helmet away and soothed me back into peace. The years blurred my vision, and I don't remember if I was screaming. When I had grown, I asked what that event was. My contacts said it was a device that measured my psychic sensitivities, as they were looking at specific frequencies I would respond to. As a child, it seemed cruel, but as an adult, it made sense. If they didn't know what 'frequency' I could detect, then psychic contact with them would be impossible.

To my recollection, one of the last in-person visitations I had as a child was being visited by the purple skin humanoid Ahntajisan. I woke unprompted to see a dark woman standing beside my bed. Her shadowed visage startled me, and she knew it. She crouched down and leant over me. I cannot recall if she instructed me or if I simply knew it was time to leave, but I reached out to clasp her hand, ready to go again. We hurried through the blue-lit window and back into a room, but this time, it wasn't a classroom. To my limited understanding, it appeared to be an art gallery that was being visited by numerous human children.

As the night slipped away from memory, the very last poignant moment before returning to my bedroom was Ahntajisan taking me to a dark hilly field. She leant down and said:

"This was the last time we will see each other like this."

I cried and sobbed into her embrace. It felt like I was saying goodbye to a parent. There was a bond that had grown between us; I wonder what sort of other adventures we had, but I curse those lost memories. When I asked what this meant many years later, my E.T. contacts told me they were satisfied with my abilities to perceive and interact with them beyond the scope of physicality. When I asked why they chose to minimise tangible contact, they said:

"Because it is safer for both of us."

Although my child's mind could not have understood this, I was assured that I was not alone – that they will still be there, just in a different way. Sure enough, the visitations continued through the astral plane.

This was around the time when I started having memories of being in unusual places as someone else. Places that I know I have not been to and bodies that were unlike my own, yet they were me. Though these were not distinct memories at this point, they were appearing as emotions and thoughts. For instance, knowing what it was like being an adult human woman – so my mother was fortunately spared the 'talk' with me. However, it would not be until several years later when I recalled my very first past life memory.

When I became an adult, my E.T. contacts did confirm they did assist with unclogging past life recalls, but their intent was for me to remember why I came here and our agreement before reincarnating. However, there was a greater reason: it was to fully realise my existence in this life on this world. Having these memories was painful, and I scolded them for not preparing me or warning me as a child. They said the pain was the key and I had to learn to coexist with these beings as I was one of them before. How can you explain that to a child?

I had travelled to them so often, that I had a favourite place. There was a realm that had tall spiral structures that broke conventional physics and shining smiles from the people who visited there. I saw a blue slide that was suspended in the air, but I noticed people entering the slide from the bottom before they were shot up into the tube and disappeared. I had to try it for myself. I floated towards it and sat steady near the bottom; I could feel water trickling around and through my body for a moment before I was sucked through into the dark.

It was so sudden it startled me, but I remember the pure bliss in this ride. I was screaming-laughing, but I couldn't hear a sound from my mouth. There was a break of light in the tube, I slipped pass and looked around the opening. I was sliding along a sun-burnt canyon; I could see the piercing sun cracking through the high and rugged walls of the cavern, and to my left, I saw an opening between the rocks to a grand desert that stretched into infinity. It was so beautiful and sudden, I soaked in every fleeting second of the view before sliding into the dark tube again.

I was shocked with joy that it numbed me. Another opening in the tube led me through an underwater world. The deep blue and the distant white light above were casting the shadows of massive creatures with long bodies and flippers. They darted away as I slid across the luminescent bed of an alien ocean. I was plunged back into the dark tube for mere moments before appearing in a vast forest. I slid along the winding tree branches as wide as footpaths. The rusty peach sunset blanketed the emerald and violet leaves on the canopies to the horizon. That view, that ride – that whole moment was one of magic.

I don't know how long I was on this ride, it could have been minutes or hours, but to me it was seconds. I remember wishing it lasted forever. I was sucked through the tube before landing down into what appeared to be a water fountain. There was a splash as I tried to find my bearings; I could see people walking past, paying little to no mind to my presence. I tuned to the seemingly innocent blue tube that was the greatest waterslide in the universe. The place where I found the slide had a plethora of many rides; I recall going to a few of them as a child, and it felt like a theme park. Although I didn't know the name of it, I loved the place so much I dubbed it 'Mini Disneyland.'

Though my nights were filled with alien astral encounters, my days were abundant with visitations. I would play with my primary school friends during class breaks on a patch of dried mud and dig up clumps of clay with our fingernails, which we lovingly dubbed 'the rock farm.' There were tall trees a few meters from our farm, and every once in a while, I would see an excited extra-terrestrial face beaming back at us. I would point out to my friends and say, 'there they are!' All my friends looked and seemed excited; I recall them saying they could see them on occasion. It was open, it was accepted – for a time.

When I spoke about my nightly visits to them and their daily visits to me, I could tell their glee in my words waned, though I couldn't put a word to those early thoughts, I suspected they had begun disbelieving me and that they could no longer see them.

Dear reader, you must understand how slow and gradual this process was. To me, this was life, it was how I saw it and I couldn't comprehend life outside of my experiences, yet I wasn't so dense to realise how different I was becoming to my peers. I was talking about what I had seen and what I knew to anyone and everyone, and I trusted that those who listened trusted me. Until one day, hardness of reality bashed through the door of my experience.

My grandparents were staunch disbelievers in anything beyond the physical. They were former Yugoslavians with staunch atheistic views. I do not condemn or judge anyone's views on spirituality and esoteric; this point is only made to understand the opposing environment I was raised in – and how much harder my life became. To quote them 'if I cannot see it; it doesn't exist.' I was eight to nine-years-old when I told my grandparents about my visitors and my visits.

I argued through tears, yet they insisted my experiences were invalid – they didn't believe me when I told the truth. I ran to my pillow and cried through gritted teeth. I was distraught because I knew what I saw, and my trusted authoritarians didn't share their trust with me. My mother listened to my stories but assumed it nothing more than imaginary friends. Yet, unlike my grandparents, she let me speak and be a child. Even she condemned their words to me that day.

Despite how furious I was at my grandparents for denying my experiences, I still trusted their authority implicitly. When I finished wiping the tears away and shaking off the anger, I considered my grandfather's words. Yes, my trust in them had been compromised and I vowed to never talk to them about my E.T. friends, but their words stayed – cementing the seed of doubt.

The following weeks, months and years, I would communicate with my astral friends less and less. I remember seeing them lingering along the green oval fields of my primary school, as if they were waiting for me to involve them in my friends' games, but I didn't. Until one night, when one young astral visitor came to me. A little purple girl asked me why I don't come and play with them anymore. I tried ignoring her, turning over in my bed, pretending she wasn't there. Because she was not, that's what I was told.

She pushed and pushed, even in her silence, she wanted me to look at her. I had enough. I turned around and told her to:

"Go away! You aren't real!"

Her presence wavered and slipped away into nothingness. That was the last time I saw her and it was the last time I saw one of them. They pulled away and let me continue with my life, trying to be everyone's friend at school, to be liked and respected, trying to fit in and mix with others. I was trying so hard to fill the void in my heart where my alien friends once inhabited.

This doesn't mean I was a sad child, but I was not a happy one either. Adolescence was knocking and for so many before and

among me, the transitioning from childhood was unrelenting. I was
not the exception, barring the fact I started to recognise that
humans had anything close to real history. With that, I assumed
those E.T. experiences were old shadows of childhood and adopted
the consensus reality.

The world continued spinning; life resumed and I transitioned
into high school. I had nearly put aside my E.T. contacts entirely,
shoving those memories to the very back of my mind to focus on
growing up. However, my past life sensations, which I still could
feel lingering at the very back of my consciousness. I tried
dismissing them. I held them back like a raging river; I denied them
and assumed they were old childhood imaginations along with the
encounters with E.T.s, but I could never fully do it. These sudden
spikes of knowledge entered my head without reason, like knowing
and understanding the complexities of some intimate aspects of
adulthood, ranging from biological to emotional.

Growing up was hard, but I knew I had done this before – many
times before. It was as if I was an adult in a child's body and I had
been born already several awareness levels ahead. This state of being
stayed dormant until the proper time … waiting for the time when I
could no longer hold back the now-furious river of memories.

Section 2 – Reunion

At fourteen years old, I became a goth, I met my life-long
friends in high school, I had a handful of crushes, I said goodbye to
a friend when she moved away, I gained a stepfather, I discovered
the wonders of the internet and I hated school. This was ordinary
chaos for a young teen. Despite my seldom attendance at school, I
started learning about mental health. This was the mid two-
thousands, where people were beginning to be more open and
accepting to those who were not considered 'the norm.'

At this age, I thought that those who suffered with disorders
were more or less incapable of functioning normally and were
utterly devoid of any sense of common-sense reality. I did not

understand how wide and grey the spectrums were of what was considered as healthy or unhealthy. At fourteen, I saw only two polarising extremes: you are perfectly healthy or utterly untenable. And once anyone was seen that way, their lives and credibility were unsalvageable. I was absolutely wrong, of course, but I didn't understand this fact until many years later.

I remember that night as if it were yesterday. Strangely, the date and time are lost to history, but that night was the start of the rest of my life. I was in the middle of some forgettable dream, until a hazy crackling cloud obfuscated my view and replaced it with a new one. My eyes were transfixed on a pair of golden orbs before me. I took a moment to soak in a shimmering outline of a head, neck and shoulders, all enveloped within an aura vibrating in potent gold light. This wasn't the golden-skin lady from my childhood, this was someone quite different. However, on reflection, this face was familiar.

The eyes stared back at me – through me, and though the lines of the facial features were blurred, I recognised him.

"I am Mezreth," he said.

I don't recall responding, but this image of a god-like creature halted any sense of thought or reason.

*An important note: this was a telepathic conversation. A typical linear conversation is extremely difficult to funnel via writing or verbal testimony, because of the nature of this conversation. In my previous experiences with E.T.s, like with Antajisan and the golden lady were through telepathy, there was a clear and direct language associated (they were thinking in English and used the English form of dialogue.) However, Mezreth was unlike all other E.T.s I had met prior or post this meeting.

Mezreth communicates not only through the receiver's understood base language, but bombs the receiver with more information – linking dozens of subjects and concepts with each response, to the point it becomes like lightning, shooting off into many relevant directions. It can take hours to disseminate and articulate every point in a linear and logical fashion, whereas with Mezreth's method of dialogue, these conversations happen within seconds.*

"I represent Aniqoa, an interstellar cooperative of many species among the stars and beyond. A council of representatives have come together, from a collection of races, to aid in humankind's time of awakening to the Greater Community. We have been seeking the right people to be our representatives for the right time, and we believe that you may be that one of many. This is an opportunity for you to understand us and your (and humanity's) future…" he said.

Dear reader, I would fail to describe to you how I felt at this moment. In this litany of emotions, ranging from shock and disbelief, to awe and wonder, my history burst forth from the dam and flooded my present.

Mezreth seemed to sense my reawakening, "but most importantly, this is an opportunity to understand your past. However, if you wish to continue with your life in peace, then when you wake, this meeting will only be a dream."

With his offer, this had birthed my purpose. I accepted.

I felt his pull through to his plane, as if I had been sucked into an ethereal portal. My senses wandered around the landscape; I saw the blinking stars in the sea of black and the pristine teal curve of a world beside me. I was so charged and alive, but a part of me knew that a part of me remained snug back in my bedroom.

Mezreth's yellow figure floated among the black background. I knew this was space, I knew I was looking at earth, and I knew I had experienced this many times before. The sensations were identical to my travels to 'Mini Disneyland' and a plethora of many other wonderous travels.

"This is astral travelling," Mezreth said.

"So, they weren't dreams?" I asked.

"Some were dreams; some were not. You have been able to astral travel your whole life," he said.

I glanced to earth. "Am I the only one who can?"

"All beings can, but if one lives among those who are not aware and assume it away as a dream, then how can one ever be?" he said.

"How can I tell the difference between this and a dream?"

"Simple," Mezreth said as he pointed to the silvery crescent moon in the distance, "if you are in doubt, summon an object in a room that cannot exist, like a whole moon inside of a bedroom. In dreams, your deep consciousness can break the laws of reality at whim. But in your astral form, you are just an observer and are still bound to conventional reality."

I wondered at that moment how normal this is for them to have such a simple answer to one of the most debated abilities in human history. Of course, this led to ten thousand more questions, but I got the feeling that a mere handful would be answered over the course of my life.

Mezreth beckoned me towards the moon. It looked so far away, but the longer I stared at it, it seemed as if the moon moved towards us incredibly quickly, or we moved at blinding speed towards it. We drifted around the dark side, down under its shadow, until several lights twinkled into view. There appeared to be rivers of light tracing around the darkest corners of the moon: there was life. Mezreth and I dove deep into the surface, so deep we travelled through the rocks and structures until we came upon artificial caverns and long corridors. They were filled with people, all kinds of people – beyond my imagination.

We finally came upon a dark circular room. The sparkling floor was the deepest beryl I have ever seen with beautifully etched markings that encircled the entire chamber. It appeared to represent the earth in 2D form, like an observation room – but who was observing, I wondered. I could see figures just behind the shadowy curtains; their faces brightened when they saw me as they stepped into the downcast of light.

The first few had purple skin, then others had a glowing blue, then gold, then green, then red – there were dozens of different humanoids.

"They are the Ashtar Council, a socio-political group that makes contact," Mezreth said.

I soaked this moment in, trying to capture the many strange faces around me. I wanted to know more, I wanted to know everything about them – about us. I don't recall if there were any discussions, it was such a blur of thoughts and emotions swirling around me that words and memory fail. However, I do recall what happened the following morning.

I found myself back in my physical body, waking up in my cosy bed, I felt rejuvenated and breathless – begging to a mightier power that it was not a dream. But I woke up with something else that I had never experienced before. I remember hearing their thoughts while I was in my astral form, but they carried over into my waking state. I could hear a distant murmur of minds in the very back of my head, and I realised I became bonded with Mezreth and the Ashtar.

In the following days, weeks and months, I was able to overhear so much of their conversations while (on the odd occasion) I was at school and home. I was not only hearing their minds, but when I closed my physical eyes, I could 'see' their faces and bodies standing in that dark room within my mind's eye. I could see them, and they could see me.

Mezreth is my guide and the closest thing I
can fathom to a god, though he
vehemently rejects such a title. He is calm
and all-knowing, because he wrote the
script.

Sazla is an eternal being that sits behind
every diplomatic and covert mission
involving Earth. If Mezreth were a hand;
she is the mind.

Shshmrnashsh is a being made; not born. They were designed to act, until they became aware.

Vern was an experiment made by flesh-
crafters to break away from the cold
synthetic shell of their ancient
civilisation.

Ouro believed being a psychic therapist
was his calling, until he felt the call to
become warden of the void, until he heard
his true calling before settling as an
ambassador.

Treneer was never attached to her weak
body, her mind soared far into ephemeral
astral planes to grow, until her eyes
wandered over to a small, pearly blue
planet.

Lensyann is a breathing embodiment of
science. The universe is written in a
mathematical language, that she has spent
millennia to decode.

Ahn'kat was never meant to do to
anything other than manage a failing
empire. However, he felt there was
another place that needed the wisdom,
and failures of his kin.

Neobatri always believed her place was with her kin, every role she was placed in was to aid her empire. Her being a former infiltrator, allowed her to know many things beyond the station of her peers.

Gosog wanted to break the cycle of age and decay, so, he became obsessed with transferring consciousness within machines. Now that his fears no longer grip him, he wants to ease those with similar fears.

Luanda was a healer, but her warmth was
reserved only for those she tended to.
Though, she has no love for people, she
feels obligated to bring rejuvenation.

Cintas was a exo-planar explorer, but most
of her adventures were done in a small,
isolated laboratory. In her older centuries,
she adores nothing more than being in loud
rooms and meeting strange people.

Zenik is old, but his distain for the wicked
burns hotter than youth's. After a
devastating loss, he pursed questionable
justice until he was given a chance for
redemption.

Baylan was a voluntary test subject, or dare
devil, until an injury ended her passion.
However, there is one place (and people) she
dares to engage with.

Rem is a recent 'reawakened.' Their consciousness remained in the machine for eons, reaching limits of every imaginable thought. Despite their artificially drawn out life, they missed what it felt like to be in a moving body.

Marro, the 'Golden Lady,' has worked with
hundreds of human children and crafted
them into contactees.

Volaris Jiri Manith is no amateur to difficult
and ignorant species. Her relaxed demeanour
and genuine curiosity can disarm, even the
most stubborn. She cannot tell a joke to save
her life.

Anzimo and Plutko two species but are symbionts. He has alluring charisma, but his counterpart, the plant-man, does the thinking for them both.

Antajisan, 'the Purple Lady.' She has been my second guide and teacher in this life. I regard her as my other mother – from another planet.

N'renatchi (Rena) and Wissimiru are also symbionts. They possess fine acuity but have a no-nonsense attitude – especially in politics.

Kynthbalen is a quiet one, despite his
people's fiery reputation. He sits behind
every meeting and conversation and notes
the welfare of those working too close to
Earth.

.

Sarenyth. Whatever your assumptions are of this image of this man is likely the correct one.

Savan mastered verbal sparring when she was denied entry at a stylist college. Her sharp tongue and judgement of appearances has earnt her enemies as a delegate, but she goes by this code: "people love showing their true selves in their garments, you just have to know what to look or look out for."

Tudvik was born in the wilds, far from
civilisation, but the call of meeting new
species came when he was attacked by an
otherworldly entity. He has never fully
recovered, but he cautiously wants to
understand unusual minds.

Sorrell is not someone I have ever spoken with, but I have felt her presence among the delegates. And they always seem unnerved when she comes.

Bunjalo became a hardened soul when he was forced into war between his kin and their oppressors. After decades of reunification and repentance from the other side, his heart softened enough to be in the same room as them.

Tzjasi is a huntress of the deeps, but when she
and her kin found ancient structures borrowed
deep in the blacks of the ocean, she knew there
was more to this universe than what she was
led to believe.

M'gtha is a name I will never be able to
pronounce without bleeding, but she
wouldn't take offence if you get it wrong,
only if you whimper or are soft spoken.

Tak was born on a failed colonial world.
Order was left to the individual and his days
were spent struggling to see tomorrow. He
managed to get away, but never forgot his
early brutal lessons.

Surugar is an uncut gem. His eerie silence and
stoic stare can unnerve strangers, but after a
while, he takes quiet pleasures in the smallest
of things. He would be your best friend even
if neither of you exchanged a word.

Herwinjasa was raised by her tiny town like
the other children, none of them knew their
parents, since every adult was their parent.
She now seeks to expand her tribe to an
interstellar level.

I don't know the name of this being, but I
have seen them lingering around the lunar
base. His skin is rough, but he is a mammal –
just scale-likeskin.

I don't know the name of this being, nor have I seen them in my astral visitations. I was given a mental image of these beings from my other contacts. They live in the deep black waters of other worlds and are considered more fish than mammalian.

I don't know the name of this being, but I have seen him attend conversations with the other Ashtar. Despite his appearance, he's in his teens and is in the process to be a replacement for someone who is aging too quickly (Surugar.)

To some cultures, smiling can be a
threatening gesture. Fortunately, this one is of
pure joy and welcoming.

Never met them, nor do I know their name,
but I have seen them in my mind's eye. This
is a depiction of an Arinu Elder.

I don't know the name, nor have I met this being, but I have been shown in my mind's eye some of the outrageous and awe inspiriting clothing from Arinu. I believe this is another Elder.

This was the most amazing image I have seen
in my mind's eye. I have never met them, nor
do I know their name, but I was shown how
magnificent Arinu Grand Elder's look like.
This one looks like they can break worlds
with their mind.

When the Zanashj Empire reached its heights,
they sent out malleable infiltrators to every
desirable world they wanted to conquer. These
infiltrators would take the visage and persona of
targeted leaders, destroy the planet's economy so
they would be too weak to resist conquest.
Thank the universe they don't do this anymore.

I don't know the name of this being, but I think he was a notable hero for the Zanashj.

Don't let appearances fool you, Zanashj can
live to several thousand years.

When I asked my Zanashj contacts who led them, this was the image they send me into my mind's eye.

Xannians have a strong bond with their
world, some take spiritual across the desert
wastes to achieve what is needed – not
necessarily wanted.

I believe this Xannian woman's name is
Sebima. I have never spoke to her, but I have
felt her presence when calculating possibly
future outcomes of Earth. Perhaps its good
thing we never spoke.

I have been given the profile of this being many times over the years. I don't know their name, but I believe they might be in a place of authority for Xannians.

The Ezoni celebrate for a week in the middle
of every season. There's the Blooming
Festival, Flame Festival, Shying Festival and
then the Death Festival. Celebrants wear
inhuman masks during the Death Festivals.

It was not long after that night, I rekindled with a familiar face: Ahntajisan. I was overjoyed that she was not a figment of my imagination, even though a part of me was embarrassed at my refusal to acknowledge her when I was a child. I remember when visiting during my astral travels, she and I would sit on a teal and emerald patch of grass overlooking an alien city in the distance. She was downloading (telepathically educating) information on how to harness and sharpen my Third Eye, an astral sensor responsible for psychic ability. One of the earliest lessons was how to attune my Third Eye's 'lenses' to detect auras.

"That's so boring! If telekinesis and mind control is possible, then why don't you teach me that instead," I told her once.

"Well, you need to start somewhere. If you want to run, you need to learn how to stand," she said in so many words.

No matter how much I begged her and Mezreth to bestow superpowers on me, they never did – perhaps because they already knew how much damage a teenage girl could do even without creating fire with her mind. With their teachings, I was able to see and read auras, certain electro-magnetic fields and perceive them when they were around me. However, the list continued into a particular ability that I began to favour out of all others: telepathy.

It started off with being able to read my contact's surface thoughts, but with more practise I started to expand it to earthly animals and sometimes humans. I was getting very, very good. However, I started to believe I was a higher being – I felt greater than all those around me. This cancerous arrogance grew enough for Mezreth to notice.

He had always been patient; he was my mentor and friend, but I felt I had hit a boundary with him. Mezreth saw a shadow looming over and gave me this warning:

"You may have an extraordinary life, but you are not above anyone of them. You are the right person, for the right time – that is all."

I shelved that warning. If he and Ahntajisan were teaching me to awaken these abilities, how could they expect that I should be an equal to my peers? I grew detached from my family and friends; when I would see strangers, I would smirk thinking how clueless they were – how their small lives paled to the vastness of this universe. If contactees were part of the magnificent future of humankind, then what place did the unenlightened have in that future? None, I thought.

My coldness towards humanity grew, and it was not slow as I watched news report, after news report. Murder, cruelty, destruction, apathy – this was culmination of the worst aspects of human nature and was only getting worse by the day. If they insist on destroying themselves, I thought, then what do you do when you encounter a rabid dog?

I won't lie, dear reader. These dark thoughts have never fully left me, but I like to believe nearly fifteen years later, I have been moderated – thanks to Mezreth. He made it clear that these ideas were not acceptable, out of concern it would stun any hope of whatever my future role would be. So, he took away the one thing that started this nasty spiral: my telepathy. Not only did he blur telepathic senses, but he added another thing that would make this lesson memorable: psychic empathy (not to be confused with psychological empathy).

I had not noticed it at the beginning, but when I would try to focus on particular people or even read the minds of family and friends, I was met with a static mess. A little while after that, it had almost become silent from even my pets' minds. The only constant thoughts were from my contacts. Then an achy pained feeling would crawl into my consciousness; it was something unexpected and definitely unwanted. When I would see people in distress, it would hurt even more. Even when I was alone, I had those overwhelming feeling that compressed over my chest, as if the emotional weight of the world had finally found a person to fall on. I demanded to know what was going on, but Mezreth didn't reply. He knew I understood what this was and why this was happening.

I reflect on this experience as an adult. It was one of the most important lessons I have ever learnt from my contacts: forget the illusion that we, contactees, are special. Our experiences, though not conventional among the human populace, does not allow us to assume we are above all others who do not have them. It's either every single being's experience is special or not one single being's is. Now, I believe in the former. It's a fine, grey line we have to walk – otherwise, people like Mezreth would not be able to fill an egotistical cup with knowledge.

However, even with these awesome changes, I still had doubts. Despite how awe-inspiring my experiences were, I was also incredibly conflicted with doubt. How could I not be? I was speaking to family and friends about my E.T. friends, some accepted it – while others did not. I was not a child anymore, so their doubts could no longer overtake my growing assertion of reality, but I understood why they were sceptical. Sadly, it still hurt, but I quickly learnt when and how I should reveal this information to those special few.

I wanted to prove it, but all my tangible experiences were through astral or psychic means. When I hear about people researching E.T.s, they talk about crop circles in their gardens or strange metallic implants inside their bodies. I began begging my contacts to come meet my parents, to show them what I had been living, but none came. Then that horrid question came, what if I was sick? What if these experiences were delusions of some kind, a psychosis?

The thoughts murmuring in my mind, the visions of E.T. astral forms, my astral travels – everything I had experienced came into the scary possibility of being an expression of an insanity. I was barely fifteen when these fears crawled in, and I was plunging into loneliness. After a nasty argument I had with some closest to me, I ran out to the street and kept running before dropping to the concrete and sobbing. The argument did not involve my experiences, but the stresses of that time built to a crescendo before breaking.

Suddenly, I could hear the Ashtar's voices become louder as if they had turned up their volume. This made the chaos of emotions drop for a moment as I listened. They heard my distress and responded. One of the first individuals who came to me was Tudvik. Tudvik was always distant in the beginning, but now he was at the forefront. I saw his childhood flash into my mind's eye, the dry arid world he had grown to know and love, his family and the many mistakes he has made over his long life. He had given me a present to know who he was and how he came to be in the Ashtar. Then, it was Savan's turn. I lived the memories of her life – she had never intended to go down the path of xeno-politics but found her calling here.

One-by-one, I was given the most amazing retelling of these foreign people's lives. In a moment, the division of myself – of humanity – and these E.T.s was gone, and the only thing left was this commonality: they were people. Indeed, they had incredible power, technology and vast awareness, but they were only people. I felt their love and hate, fight and combine. Their souls were in equal turmoil as much as our own. It was at that moment that I realised the human condition was not exclusive to humans.

This lightning strike of the information left me spinning and burdened with determination. This rapid pile-up of information would have taken a lifetime if it were simple imagination – this was proof to me. I was no longer in doubt of these beings and I needed to tell their story to everyone.

Section 3 – Past Lives Remembered

The past refuses to be forgotten. No matter how hard one tries, it always sits there – simmering just below the surface. When E.T.s returned to my life, I was in awe of them, and I wanted to know everything about their society and history. But there was another history I needed to know. Mezreth and Antajisan were carefully encouraging me to reconnect to my past life memories, because they wanted me to understand why and how I came to be in this time and this incarnation.

They never said I had lived before, and they never said who or what I was – even if I asked. My contacts never told me the details.

"My testimony will contaminate your true memories," Mezreth said.

I was frustrated, but I understood. He wanted me to organically let them in, and I did. Remember: I did not have a lead on who, what, when or where I was before this life – until one night.

I was in a dream. At this point, I had learnt to distinguish an astral travel experience versus a conventional dream, but this was something unlike I had felt before. I was surrounded by people, swarms of panicked people running through a white, burning city. I felt my heart thumping, I felt the electrifying heat, the cold dread and the horrid realisation that I was going to die.

I watched through the eyes of another person, exiting a building and walking over to a marble balcony and seeing death in the distance. A burning violet sphere expanded over the horizon, engulfing the grass, houses, streets and people. The mountains and hills vanished from the light, and the land itself was shaking and cracking open, swallowing all on its surface. The sphere of energy came so quickly; I couldn't move fast enough. Not that I could, as my legs and torso were fixed as stone. I remember electricity running across my scalp and between my hair strands as I watched death come. It hit me in the face and I was then met with black.

I could hear my own thoughts in this blackness, repeating in shock 'I'm dead, I'm dead, I'm dead.' What broke my thoughts were my realisation that I was still thinking, I still had some semblance of consciousness. I cannot be dead if I am still here. I could feel the blackness waning away, revealing over strange misshapen objects of unimaginable colour taking form. I was no longer in any place that resembled reality; I was in a place where all exit and enter life.

I snap awake in my bed. I was shaking as the final images of that 'dream' echoed in my head. The vision of this alien landscape after the energy sphere had slipped from my memory. As if my surface brain could not comprehend or compare it to anything it has tangibly experienced before, but it could recognise a body standing

110

on ground among a city and feeling unimaginably afraid. When I woke up that morning, I had my very first past life memory, and it was the moment I died.

The memory haunted me, it still does the more I dwell on it and try to recall every tangible detail of that experience. I came to Mezreth, to seek answers and some comfort.

"It's no wonder you are so shaken. Remembering past incarnations, while living, is difficult. The brain is limited to how much knowledge it can hold. The soul is infinitum, whereas its incarnations, are not. Each life is brief for that reason. A memory of intense emotions are the keys to unlock doors of your previous lives. The moment of your death had scarred your soul, but you could not remember your past life without it," he said.

"Did I have more lives? Were they just as bad?" I asked. I was hesitant at the idea of remembering more horrible things. If this is what past lives were – I wanted to forget, at least for this lifetime.

"Like all, you had many lives! Just because you remember the ugly, does not mean there was no beauty," he said.

And with that, I let them flow into my surface mind. The second handfuls of memories came showing the life before my death, like life was going in reverse. There were sprinkles of odd memories here and there, some events that seemed to hold no meaning without context. It took me years to figure out how old I was in that life when experiencing those scenes, trying to piece a chronological story of that powerful past incarnation. Now, I know who I was.

Fifteen-thousand years ago, I was Delta Ungbrahe, born to wealthy socialites in the Atlantean era – the closest thing humankind came close to a Golden Age. And gold it was for many millennia. I was a scholar that had fallen in love with history and had an excellent memory to recall the finest details of our and the world's history.

I remember reading about the beginning: the birth of civilisation began from struggle for survival. In a time more ancient than the Atlanteans, the world was bleeding in war and chaos. Nations fought with nations, forests burned, children taught to kill strangers and die for their supreme lords. A group of stragglers stood up against this doomed path and said enough. From opposing sides, these survivors came together to escape.

They knew of one land that was untouched by war, unsullied by madness, but it was a mystery even to them. This land was known as Atlantia. There was hardly anything known about that land. Out of the hundreds of brave explorers that ventured there, barely a handful returned. The ones that did, spoke of the island-continent sat in the centre of a vast ocean, surrounded by nigh-invisible mists and treacherous coral and rocks littering around her shores.

Out of bravery and desperation, the survivors stole ships, equipment, food – anything they could grab before making the voyage to the mists. Some ships didn't make it, people died from disease or starvation, and the enveloping mists made some ships utterly disappear. After long and terrifying months, they finally saw the grey outline of mountains to the horizon. Elated, the survivors hurried over, but took care navigating the rocks below the water's surface.

Their hands dug into the dusky wet sands when they reached land. Their salvation was almost upon them, but they realised they knew nothing of this place. As the newcomers slowly built encampments, their bravest voyaged into the woods. They were pleasantly surprised to find the land was rich in wood and bamboo, many large caves, minerals and edible vegetation. However, as much there was splendour, there was equal danger.

The land was rife with deadly wildlife that had a taste for flesh, cave bears and hulking tree-cats; even the plants were predators. Some had needle-like spikes coated in a paralytic poison, and if one was unlucky enough to get cut, their bodies would be consumed very, very slowly. The newcomers became afraid to leave their camps and some even wanted to return to their old kingdoms. Unbeknownst to them, they were not alone.

There were humans already living on Atlantia for many millennia. They studied the newcomers before carefully approaching and offering them some guidance. The newcomers were thrilled but questioned why were natives showing such compassion to strangers. The answer was simple: the true Atlanteans understood their home's deadly nature and they understood if they were to survive, they had to stay together. That meant they would do no harm to each other and all conflicts were settled civilly. They had a love for their kin.

As time progressed, unity formed between the two. The marriage of advanced technology and advanced spiritual ideals strengthened the unity between them. However, they believed there was a chance that the old warlords will track them and bring strife onto the shores of Atlantia. So, the first generation of the Atlantean civilisation was formed, and its beginning was called the Age of Fear. Atlanteans constructed wonderous military defences; every civilian became a militia, and every corner of the land became a stronghold to hold invasions. Not only was military technology and tactics developing rapidly, but there was an explosion of other advancements, like medicine, infrastructure and communication.

For many generations they expected invaders and, the Atlanteans finally realised no one had come to their shores to attack them. When they ventured beyond the mists to the old cities that their ancestors spoke of, they had only found ruins and craters. These kingdoms, nations, and whole civilisations had wiped themselves out. Atlanteans were horrified believing that they were the last of humanity, but they could not have been any more wrong. Deep in the forests and high in the mountains, small clusters of humans still lived in isolation, far away from the 'haunted' ruins of their past.

Atlanteans were elated and quickly realised they had an opportunity to ensure, not only survival but the evolution of humanity. With their spiritual and technological teachings, they carefully approached each group and slowly laid a foundation. Over centuries, Atlanteans successfully "seeded" every society on earth they came across, barring the Lemurians.

Atlanteans revered the Lemurians and learnt greatly from their spiritual teachings. Atlanteans even tried offering some of their technological capabilities, but unlike all the others, the Lemurians refused. Atlanteans respected life, but it was not until the Lemurians who taught us:

"No matter stone or flesh, if it has a soul; it is alive and it has rights."

We dedicated laws to this reality and adhered to it. Time passed and eventually the connection between these great peoples was severed. It has not been recorded, but some ancient tales repeated that the Lemurians saw a shadow in the Atlanteans. Since then, the Atlanteans were banned from the red lands to the eastern south.

It was not long after that E.T.s made contact with humans, reasoning that humanity was now ready to join the interstellar community. We were developing at a rapid pace, even rivalling some of our off-world neighbours. We had whole schools dedicated to learning psionics and vast population were psychic. We even had ceremonies and laws around psychic conduct. Things had never been better and the future was bright with prospects, a world without strife or senseless suffering, a true Golden Age for humanity and those in the stars. But, they were all wrong.

It's hard to say when things fell apart. There was no singular event that led Atlanteans to the shadow the Lemurians eluded. I believe it was a grey spectrum with thousands of bad choices that toppled into the next. Afterall, Atlanteans were still humans.

As the heart of Atlantia rotted, the surface remained pristine. In the land of psychics and scholars, none knew how decayed things became, because they believed it could not happen. Out of all our crimes, the greatest one was when Atlanteans fell in love with their own legend. It blinded us to our friends, neighbours and darkening path.

I was born into the last generation, but of course, we were all oblivious to it. My soul reincarnated as a being who was less remarkable than the average citizen. I was a mundane, I lacked psychic ability and I was targeted by peers and even some family. Do not assume I took their abuse without violent consequence against my bullies. Sometimes, I also retaliated against my teachers and friends. My parents were well-known, wealthy and incredibly psychically gifted, but they (particularly my mother) were embarrassed to have a mundane child. I was considered "psi-disabled" by my own community and they gave me their pathetic pity. I was fed up.

It was not long when I was exiled from home to find my own way in life. Although, I had no psychic ability, I still had my mind and ambition. My early years were rough, but I was not entirely alone. I had my lavender bird, A'gesh that kept by my side as I found myself. I became an archivist who worked in the library of Capihul city, and my colleagues were independent researchers and scholars who recorded culture, science, wisdom-keeper knowledge and countless more subjects.

I was tasked to collect data from a crystal powerplant nearby Capihul one day. What I learned that day changed my life.

Shortly before my birth, humanity was going through an energy shortage crisis. We had large generators that siphoned useable energy to power our homes and many other endeavours. However, they were sorely outdated and Atlanteans were accelerating scientific and engineering research, which maxed out the old generators. We subtly began clamping down energy flow on other countries and began hoarding it for ourselves. Why? Because Atlanteans were beginning to obsess with how far humanity could climb the technological ladder. But in doing so, we discarded our spiritual evolution.

Atlanteans wanted to construct better ways to control natural disasters and protect places, even ways to defend themselves against possible interstellar incursions. We were desperate not to be left behind all the others. While we were designing the next generation of energy generators and pylons, we had something to supplement our needs for the meantime. Over our many exchanges, humans had learnt that some highly advanced E.T. species used unique crystals for ceremonies, psychic rituals, improvement of mental abilities and connecting with the universe.

The only thing that caught our attention was the amount of power these crystals possessed. We went out and mined them from black crusts of dead worlds near the centre of the galaxy and brought them back for immediate use and study. Sadly, these temporary measures became conveniences. Overnight, the energy crisis was averted, and everyone stopped talking about it. When the greater interstellar community discovered what we were doing, they warned us to stop – we were told we were not ready for this and that those crystals were misused. We ignored them, we told them they were not our wardens and that we had a right to do what all others could do.

The E.T. delegates understood they could do nothing to change our minds, but they could compel their own citizens who lived and worked on earth to return to their homes. I remember being a child, seeing E.T. people working as merchants and teachers; they were friends and some were family. We had become so integrated that we were utterly desensitised to their presence. However, as I slowly grew into a woman, I saw fewer and fewer off-worlder faces until it was just a sea of humans.

When I was called to survey the powerplant, where one of these crystals was kept, I finally understood the great answer to the questions I, nor my peers, had never considered. For the first time in that life, I was grateful to be mundane, because it compelled me to look behind the veil of deceit. The engineers and scientists there were evasive when I asked questions, and I did not need to be psychic to know I was unwanted there. I was approached by a worker who quietly showed me the truth.

Door after door, narrow walkway after walkway, he finally led me to the heart of the facility, where the crystal was kept. When he opened the thick metal door, light washed over us. I could barely see the outline of the fist-sized crystal suspended in the centre of the tiny chamber. However, I noticed the closer we approached it, the energy disturbances became extreme. I was met with the thought that it behaved like a caged tiger.

The worker explained that these crystals have been subjected to intense electric pulses to extract their incredible power. This was fairly common knowledge among the scientific community, but what they or the greater community didn't know, barring those working closely with the crystals, was that they possessed consciousness. They had souls and they were alive. We trapped them in there, abused them and they hated us. We forfeited our own souls when we broke our most sacred laws. At that moment, I had no idea what we were anymore. We lied to ourselves about our identity.

I demanded to know why this was kept hidden and allowed to continue, and heartbreakingly, the answer was simple.

"If we don't do it, they will find someone else who will," he said.

When I returned to the library, I told my overseer and peers what I have learned. I was deluded to think that there would be an alert and public outcry, but I was met with a similar simple and pathetic reply:

"If it works, it doesn't need fixing."

I was devastated, but I had no power. I was just a civilian and on top of that a mundane. This collective apathy infected me after a while, too. I became a prisoner to my community. I continued with my hollowed life, all the while I tried to do one thing I never could: forget.

The truth weighed me down to the bottom until I was left with two options: wither away or do something. I was brave for a moment after what felt like a lifetime of being a coward. After enough conversations and persuasions between my most trusted colleagues, we came up with a plan to notify the right people that could possibly spread to the right channels.

I arrived at the library with my pet bird A'gesh perched on my shoulder to meet with my peers. It was an unassuming day, I even felt excitement at the idea of doing something grand under the surface. I suppose that's how those in charge felt every day. As we settled in, A'gesh started flapping. She flew around in circles, squawking so loudly it caused a scene. I tried settling her down, trying to summon her back to my arm, but she lunged at me. I reacted and swatted her out of the air before she dropped.

I felt my heart stop as I watched her rise and take off through the closest open window. She has never done that before, and I didn't have a second to process what it meant until I felt the deep vibrations. They came in waves, each wave becoming louder and more powerful until the sleek stone walls started shaking. People started rushing, and I questioned if this was an earthquake. Impossible, I thought. We haven't had any since we installed the tectonic regulators deep in the volcanoes along the centre of the country. It was significantly worse: it was our day of reckoning.

I ran out of the library and spotted a blinding sphere of energy coming beyond the hills – from the same location as the powerplant. There were a dozen other plants dotted around the country, each one now detonating the once sleeping volcanoes. It was the moment of my end. All my hopes, my evolution, any wonder of who I would become, were snatched away as I saw the wave sear every living thing from the surface. The earthquakes snapped open the ground, readying to swallow the rest of the land. The seas close to the city rushed in to wash us away. It was as if the earth herself was ripping off the Atlantean tumour.

The last thing I remembered was playing with A'gesh outside on a green hill. Watching her circle around and jump on my arm. One pure moment before I met black.

When I remembered Delta and her journey, it changed my life as Lea. I cannot remember the finest and worst moments without pain. I felt as if Delta's life – my life, was stolen from me. I was betrayed and lost any semblance of justice. Whenever I invoked her memories, I could feel her spirit screaming. I thought she wanted to live again, reclaim the life that was taken through me, but she was not crying for that.

There is a reason why I remember her story and why Mezreth and other contacts tried so hard to get me to remember those previous lives. It was to serve as a warning for today. These memories are a horrid reminder of the price of greed and misuse of power. The Atlanteans may have had the brightest potential, but it was hijacked by the wrong people making the wrong decisions.

We lost our empire then and if we do not change, we will lose the world now. Delta was incarnated in the last generation to capture the essence of the Atlantean civilisation and remember to not repeat her and our species' mistakes. My higher self knew the events that were to transpire, and I chose to be an immortal library of the ancient past for the distant future. When I connected this truth, Delta's screams stopped.

When I think about the most amazing things in this universe, it's not E.T.s' connection with humans, or their wonderful technology, or their unique cultures, or their breath-taking worlds. It is a fact that life is one of many phases and with each new incarnation, there's an endless possibility of where to go and who you will become. You are forever adding on to the endless encyclopaedia of your soul and in each life, serving for the next.

For the first time I understood, Delta died for Lea.

Where is the Empirical Proof?
Steve Strong

Of all the paranormal off-shoots none are as tenuous and questionable as channelling. It can be the most dodgy and easy to fake, and the theatrics, changing of voice and gestures all add up to something so easy to manufacture and so difficult to validate. Once we found that our research was leaning more and more towards the mystical side of the human equation, we made a conscious decision to steer clear of all that claim to be channelling. It is not that we completely dismissed this form of esoteric interaction, but more a matter of there being many proven cases of fakery and little if any of these acts of channelling are supported by empirical proof.

One Degree of Separation

My ambivalence remained set in stone until I met a lady by the name of Valerie Barrow, who claimed to be channelling an Original (Aboriginal Australian) spirit she called Alcheringa. As to whether she actually was in contact was never proven, but what I did know in absolute terms was her integrity and honesty. What I did know was that she absolutely believed she was able to pass on this spirits observation and wisdom. The book she wrote called *Alcheringa* was exceptionally insightful, and in combination with her integrity left the channelling door slightly open.

A few years on I met Lea when she spoke at a conference in Rye (Victoria). Her talk centred on Alien contacts she had, what they looked like via her portrait drawings, and more importantly, the knowledge they possessed. What was shared related directly to the Earth-bound residents; this was both unknown and unheard of by me but seemed to fit together so well with our research in recent times. Now this time around Lea was not actually channelling a departed spirit but was in actual conversation with a being fully alive and reasonably close by. All in all, it was a great presentation and had even more sensational content, but where is the empirical proof? This was all based on her subjective version of events. Just as it was with Valerie, as convincing as her rendition of events and words were, I needed more.

Testing the 'Waters'

Lea often made mention of her principal off-world guide and mentor Mezreth. Her take was that he knew virtually everything about everything, and that was my 'get out of jail card.' If he was that omniscient then my reasoning was that I could ask him questions via Lea that have answers she could not possibly know. That would satisfy my conditioned rational sensibilities beyond any reasonable doubt.

Over the next two weeks I asked ten questions; they were very obscure, but remote as the chance was, could be known. The last two questions related to personal issues and the last one I had shared with no-one, not even my wife. A probability that Lea could answer the first nine was infinitesimally possible. But the last correct answer was the 'final straw.' From that point on my stance was no longer about proving or convincing, but all about passing on the truth.

Having said that, I must include one recurring equivocation. I have never seen, met or even made contact telepathically with Mezreth. I have to 'fess up' that there were moments of questioning and second-guessing, but on each occasion, I reminded myself of another more pressing and incontestable truth. It is a simple matter of reading some of Mezreth's comments and the doubt immediately vanishes. And that is my recommendation to the reader, even they have every right to question whether Lea is lying or deluded. The only way to decide whether this process she is involved in is legitimate is to read what is claimed to be his response to the questions I raise. Once doing that we suggest you ask the same question I also entertained when momentarily lapsing into bouts of doubt: Is it possible that any mortal living on this planet could know so much and express it more eloquently and succinctly?

My answer is no. You may agree or disagree, but if you think along the same lines then, there is the possibility that what comes next will change, clarify and reconfigure so much of what you think you know about 'what, why and who'.

What comes next is replete with empirical proof, more than enough to satisfy our requirements ten times over. My understanding is that as benevolent Aliens are forbidden from making direct contact with humans until the change, they are using Lea as an interlocutor and human 'relayer' of the wisdom, knowledge and personal changes needed to be able cope with the oncoming change in earthly vibration and circumstances. If accepting Mezreth's counsel, when the Schumann Resonance permanently vibrates at an incredibly high frequency each soul and body can accommodate or be overwhelmed by discordance, the path forward he sets out becomes clearer leading towards being able to cope and remain.

The three truths that resonate through these conversations which need to be both appreciated and absorbed are that Lea is genuine, Mezreth is offering every incarnated soul the way forward and the time of global change is nearly upon us. Whether you stay or have to leave is your choice, but if you want to make a fully informed choice, the best thing you can do is to continue reading. After that it becomes progressively easier, and before you know it your continuance of tenure on this planet will be confirmed.

Transcript One

Steve:

I know E.T.s are here, but why would they bother to come here?

Mezreth:

We have been here since day one. It's a mixture of parental compassion as well as honouring certain alliances of ancient past. Humans have been in contact with us for a very, very long time. We believe humans have the potential to reclaim those old times, to reclaim those old ways to survive these new days. Humans have a mixture of resentment for the old, but there's also a fear of the new. Constant fear and constant anxiety will only ever lay down a path of darkness. We are trying to change that.

Steve:

Now what I'm getting out of that is it's not so much coming here as they were here before we were. And they've seen now in our growth at least 15 hominids running around 300,000 years ago and found another hominid in China a couple of days ago which has got a much bigger brain than ours. So somehow, they chose sapiens among all the different hominids. I find it quite interesting that there is that sort of parental link because obviously genes were crossed. Now there's two things I really want to see if we can cover. One's the ceremony, and the other is the Schumann Resonance. Mezreth is aware that ceremony took place at Uluru. And we were given a minimum number of participants which I never told anyone beforehand that we had to reach, which we exceeded by nearly fifteen million. I've got a suspicion E.T.s had some sort of either observer or participant involvement. Well, was it successful? And if it was, what did it actually do?

Mezreth:

The ceremony was a landmark in many ways because it proved to not just humans, but to us that you can work together for a common goal. And when humans connect, and you stick to something, you have that common desire in that moment, it has affected the planet. Can you imagine what eight billion people can create? Imagine how many strides forward you can achieve with this. It was a test, and you passed with flying colours. But there are many more challenges ahead. Can you remember that solution for the next challenge, we wonder? Fifteen million opened the door, but it takes the world to change the world.

Steve:

So, in other words, what that's done is open the door. I never actually thought that meant everything was roses. So now let's talk about the Schumann Resonance. It fluctuated massively during the December, 2020 ceremony. Were they involved with that or did humans do that? Or was that something completely independent?

Mezreth:

It was mostly you when you tuned in. At the same time, it was uncomfortable to feel its effects. Not only can you turn it up and down, but you can also balance it for yourselves. We also added our spark to it. It was a way for us to see you and you to see us.

Steve:

Well, that's quite deep actually. I think that really is something to think about in a lot of respects. Now, with the Schumann Resonance we made an issue of this and there's more of add to it. Evan showed me a read-out where for three days in a row at around about 1:00, the Schumann Resonance was shooting into the forties and fifties. And as we know, it's also gone up to 6000 on one occasion. And as we now know, it's gone up to a level beyond the measurement of any machine. Now I've heard rumours that now the Schumann Resonance is turned on, it's become a plaything for Aliens. Why is it still changing so much?

Mezreth:
The bumps and spikes will continue to ensure that you remember the lessons so we're going to keep that pressure to see if you can do it again. The ceremony was a lesson but what we are doing now is the real test. And the results of this test will prove that you can not only control the Schuman Resonance, but your fates, too.

Steve:
This is the whole point of this exercise. We know about that now. Is there a point in the near future where many souls incarnate here right now, will not be able to reincarnate on the planet because the frequency will be so high, that if they did, they'd perish on the Earth?

Mezreth:
Souls will be able to reincarnate, but few will successfully pass through. Those who recall their lessons may re-enter, but those who wilfully forget, will not. This leaves the door open for them to come back when they have.

Steve:
It's very much like I said, there were two lessons we had to get here. One was to learn about magic and love which means you're playing well in the playground, instead of spitting at each other. And the second one was to learn why we are here. The reason for everything and what seems to be clear to me from what you're saying there, is there has to be some idea of what both love and magic is. But there also has to be some real understanding of the purpose, and reason why people are here. Now, for the last question: as you said, some won't be able to incarnate back here. Some can come, some can't. As for the ones who can come back here or stay here after that

point in time, what comes next for the ones who do stay? Is there any vision for the future they have?

Mezreth:
There is nothing for those who side with fear over opportunity. Choices define existence as there is a consequence to each, even if you believe you made the right one. Like most civilizations that have come before you, you have come to a point where choice is no longer an option. Don't worry. You will overcome any challenge if you remember and work together as a group. Hearing you say that you can change is always lovely when you are safe and content, but we wonder if that will extend when you are faced with danger.

Steve:
. I think he's right because to an extent that you're going to get to a stage very soon where you think, hang on, I think I will go this way. But you won't be the making the final choice with your mind. It's your soul that will make that call. It's not down to what you've done before, what your mind thinks or what you say at that particular moment. That's not what the choice comes out of. It comes out of everything you've done up to that point. The words are immaterial. It's all so easy when everything's fine. Now everyone's making people so fearful, and we warned people long ago that this was going to happen.

Transcript Two

Steve:

We've mentioned this before, that the zebra, who have the same genetic general patterns in face, size and lifestyle – if you've seen one zebra, then you have seen them all. Whereas humans have seven million different faces, different fingerprints, height, style and everything else. Why are humans so distinguishable and unique? What is it that's different about our genes?

Mezreth:

You were moulded by many different hands over many ages, but sometimes, nature would take its course. After every million years, my kin would come and look. However, in recent times, our other children (Zanashj) had a hand in your development. They were grand and their flesh crafting was unmatched for an age, but their folly was a greed and grew too comfortable in luxury. Their influence spread across many worlds, but after one small poor choice, they became brittle and ultimately, shattered.

Steve:

That means this genetic mixture that we're talking about relates to what specifically happened with one species of human. Clearly, they've done this elsewhere. It seems to be a common practice. This is not the only place that has happened. Do the Zanashj come from here or do they come from somewhere else?

Mezreth:

Earth is not their home, but it was part of a dominion.

Steve:

So, we are a mixed bag from apes and E.Ts. The leads on to the second question which is the primary reason and long-term expectation of this type of genetic hybridization, what's the reason and expectation for it?

Mezreth:
There is no hybridization. You are already us.

Steve:
So, there's still a lot more to this revolving door. I added a note in here when he's referring to us, but he's talking about his mob when they were in the very early stages. He's talking about how they were still like us then.

(Lea adding context):
Yeah. That we were very, very similar, but that would have been billions of years ago and to further that he says to accept an alternate version of our history. So, the way it has been impressed upon me was that we are already sharing so much with them. It's almost as if it was kind of like we were just put here, we are still them, but just in another situation, in another place, time, and location. Mezreth keeps saying: "you are us, we are you - you're the set."

He's referring to the other young races. So, I mean, just because he's talking about other species, even though we have a lot in common, they have their own, if you will, pathways their own sort of unique roads, and they do travel in their own histories.

So that's still something a little bit above me, their desire to see humans achieve higher states. We're into efforts like, for instance, interstellar travel, et cetera, is all different to them. And he's talking about the others who know, that want to see an alternate, to see how we react in this alternate history. Whereas other younger races, they have their own desires as to what they want to do with us.

Steve:
That's the history we've got to discover, isn't it? The long-term purpose is for that curtain to be placed there and for us to realize

why. They work with other races for different purposes. Now this is the part I can tick off, in that there was some genetic sharing for a specific reason. Then past that point, we've got two options that are on offer.

The accepted mainstream genetic truth, that we've been told is absolutely right, which is one day a monkey mummy, and a monkey daddy made us. We crawled around on all fours, then we stood up on two legs, then we dribbled a little and then walked into a cave about 40,000 years ago.

And here we are today at the pinnacle of existence on this planet, maybe in the cosmos. That is one version and the second one is that there were earlier times and civilisations and that from the very beginning there was a melding of lines and genes. And we've had times since when we were as advanced technologically and spiritually as we are today, if not more so, then it all fell apart.

After each fall we went back to nature and became hunters and gatherers, then we stumbled back into the system of doing the same mistakes we made earlier. We hoped that the next time we're going to get it right. And we keep doing it again and again, and here we are now preparing for the next instalment. It really has to be one of the two. Our evolution is not the one we see on the science posters of us evolving from earlier hominids like Australopithecus. They are no more than a different species, a bit like all the different monkeys and different primates. So, which one was correct?

Mezreth: We will always be monkeys to our forbearers. There's no shame in it.

Steve:
I wish that was a little less cryptic. It seems that to our forebears we will always be monkeys, but with the benefit of some intriguing genetic supplements.

We know of Atlantis and Lemuria, and I don't think there's any argument that each empire existed. And if that is so, could you briefly describe their greatest achievements and inherent failings.

Mezreth:
Hubris. The taste of wonder became an addiction in our observations, even in our own time, a great civilization is the one that humbles itself and sees its own limitations before improving on them as is for the collective, as is for the soul and as is for the cosmos.

Steve:
He's talking about why it failed, which is, of course, the most important part of this equation, isn't it? Because eventually what's going to come out of this change ahead is another civilization is going to have to live together in some shape or form. Obviously, Atlantis would be the best example of what we need to guard against. And right now, we'd be vying for first place with Atlantis, wouldn't we? Moving forward, from Atlantis to Lemuria. Let's make this more specific so that we get an answer. This time I think it's going to be the same answer. I think I know the answer. Is it the same answer for both of them?

Mezreth:
Similar.

Steve:
It seems we are dealing with just a couple of minor variations of the same faults and flaws.

(Lea adding context):
But the crowning achievements became the reason they failed. They forgot what brought them here and what brought them to the highest point to the Golden Era?

Steve:
And that's interesting. I suspected even with the artifacts we've got that come from Atlantis and Lemuria, the Lemurian objects are

absolutely trustworthy and the Atlantean objects are incredibly powerful, yet so deceitful at the same time. So eventually both were blinded by their perfection.

(Lea adding context):
Yeah. And even Lemuria was blinded by their own power as well, Lemuria could see, and Atlantis perfected. So that's the crowning achievement. And I think I remember we talked about this before, that Atlanteans were obsessed with getting things correct, with getting things perfect. The rings, when they were pulsating and shining like they were, they should have been in the perfect position to assist and accelerate. But soon after Atlantis began to fall apart. But in its pure original state, it should have been a blessing, but it became a curse.

Steve:
The second ring is perfect in its geometry and its symmetry. However, the other two are both damaged. They are totally tampered with. So that was originally part of Atlantis's strength and obviously, if you take that far enough, it becomes an obsession, doesn't it?

(Lea adding context):
 It does. And with Lemuria now, I'm less familiar with Lemurian culture than I am with Atlantis. And because I wasn't Lemurian in a previous life, but Lemurians were astounding psychics. So they could see the light and magic. A crowning achievement.

Steve:
Being psychically gifted doesn't mean being flawless.

(Lea adding context):
Yeah, there is a difference. Atlanteans were also psychic but became obsessed with evolving their tech to the point where their spiritual evolution stagnated.

Steve:

That really sums up the ongoing struggle with humanity, past and present. And even to this day, we're dealing with exactly the same thing. There is a difference in the two, because that actually gets us to the hub of the difference in every one of us. I suspect to an extent the Indigenous people have carried on that Lemurian tradition of having the shaman, the mystic, the clever-fella and the Serpent whereas the other Atlantean tradition of perfection in all things sets them on a different trajectory.

And we've gone round in a circle yet again. Funny how humans haven't learned that part of it. During the ebbs and flows of what's taken place on this planet and it's been a long time, that's obvious, there have been many earlier civilizations and it sounds to me like they've always fallen into the same trap. During this time, an extensive time, what assistance and hindrance did the alien community offer as humans staggered through the destruction in Atlantis and Lemuria, what were they doing to help and guide?

Mezreth:

What we offer is chances and choices. The only hindrance is the blind fear of consequences. There is no consequence that you cannot learn from. And we will ensure you have the opportunity to do so.

Steve:

In fact, that's probably all we have to think about as it is our journey and choices. So, he offers chances and we're fearful of the consequence. Every now and then, you get a person that is stunning with ears to hear like Da Vinci or Tesla. They were not scared of the consequences, were they? They're just committed to taking the chance when it comes along. And that's the difference between nearly all of us. So that's what they've been doing.

But when you do step outside the status quo and see the real truths, it is a blessing and potential curse as one has to also control the ego and sense of importance, for if let to run free there will be consequences.

Mezreth:
All worlds are special, but a word of caution: Atlanteans also believe they were special.

Steve:
So special that they saw themselves as first amongst equals, and that is a dangerous road to navigate. What I want to discuss next relates back to the ceremony that took place, which we've agreed was actually a real thing. We don't have to go through and validate that. We know it's now only months away, what advice would he offer to humanity?

Mezreth:
Change is ugly, uncomfortable and brutal. If it's pleasant, then the wrong thing is changing and it's often the thing that will be your downfall. You have living memories that are equipped with this knowledge and understanding. Don't ask us; ask them.

Steve:
I agree such a gift and rite of passage has to be earnt, but did he then give you a specific or vague hint as to who "them" is? Are we them, or are they our souls or off-world guides?

Transcript Three

Steve:

My first question is, is it true to say that the alien race also ranges from almost ascended to uncaring and purely self-interested as many of us are today? Is that a fair call? Is that what's happened over there on the other side?

Mezreth:

Not just the species, not just social groups or movements but individuals. No two minds are the same in this universe. The Ascended are the ones who believe they are heavy, while the heavy believe they are ascended. With that: chaos is born. And wherever there is life, there is chaos. Indulge in this gift.

Steve:

So, wherever it is, life is chaos. Well, that must mean right now on this planet, we are so alive. The question that follows, because it is a now two-part question, how can this be?
Surely the more knowledgeable, the more technologically advanced and having a big picture view of everything, should theoretically make you more aware and compassionate.

That so much of the truth is hidden or stolen on this planet makes things even more difficult here. And that loss of vision and mystical purpose on this planet makes a lot of good people turn into not so good people because they don't have a big picture overview. But elsewhere most Aliens have more of these truths there for the taking. Shouldn't that lead to being selfless, less belligerent and peaceful? How is it that some of these less caring off-worlders are so ambivalent and sometimes even violent when they shouldn't be? Is there an explanation for how that could be happen?

Mezreth:

All forms of life see the universe through a single pair of eyes and judge actions based on their personal experience. It doesn't matter how high the growth of perspective somebody has, it is still within their narrow confines of their own perceptions. It doesn't matter how high they are. Even for us, the sky is the limit. It doesn't matter how rich or poor your life experiences were, management of attitude and responses to situations is vital. You will never truly 100% absolutely see the universal truth in its full entirety because you will always perceive with some bias. We have seen the whole universe and each of us emphasize different aspects. Our own values became watered down because of an abundance of time. Some of us were infected with apathy. Peaceful, yes. But we stopped wandering and became lost.

Steve:
So that's what it comes down to, it doesn't matter about your station or position. Everyone sees this story from one set of eyes, which is their own, and their own personal experience becomes part of that vision. It's a bit like this, a show some time ago, a comedy TV show, I can't remember which one, had a scene with people fighting each other, and in the background a guy was dressed up in a bear suit, he walked across the stage in the background, and no one saw it. I didn't see the bear. Everyone, maybe a dozen people were jumping all over the place. All the components were there to see, but the bear was lost in the maze.

So, when it comes down to when we see or hear a truth with our senses, it's all about how we process that truth. And in our case with everything in a state of flux, it doesn't matter whether you know more because we're still going to have a problem because there's conflict and chaos everywhere. And that's the test in this. Now, here comes the part I was interested in because a lot of those questions lead up to one fundamental universal issue.

Do all aliens believe in some form of God-like creator? And then to be specific, because I'm aware of the fact the aliens who have taken an interest in human affairs are so numerous, in this area is there a commonality in perspective and understanding of how and who created everything?

Mezreth:
Some think it's creation. Some think it's intelligence. Some think it's destruction and some think it's essence. All correct and all are Akashi. We are all garments of Akashi. Life has always been here.

Steve:
On Earth, when it comes to creation, we are told that on day one there was a massive, Big Bang Theory. That theory seems to fit some of the holes, but not all of them. In particular if there was just nothing, a limitless void of nothing, then how can nothing create everything?

(Lea giving context):
Well, what we have to understand comes through their perspective. Their consensus of what life is a little bit more broader than what we agree life is. If you ask the average person what is life, most will be exclusive nominating animals and maybe plants and some may give a more of a spiritual answer.

Another person may say it's biological. So therefore, it's this or that, so you have all these different answers. All of them are correct. They are all pieces of the whole definition of what life is. But those who have far broader perspective and who are far more learned and have explored far more areas. They would readily agree that things such as stones are just another form of life.

Steve:
I was always going to talk about that. Yes, we're on the same page that the rocks we have and what they've done, they are alive. But when people ask me, do they have a soul, I have no answer for that. But are they alive? Absolutely. Are they aware? Definitely. While I actually die. I'm not even sure they do. They just are there and continue to be.

136

This may be slightly off topic, but if we're going down this particular rabbit hole, my understanding when it comes to death, particularly when it comes to things like rocks, stones, minerals, we have seen enough to state that this is a transmutation process. Just as it is with us, just like with out with our bodies, it's a transmuted. They transmute I mean, they are pieces, they're fragments of consciousness or whatever their consciousness is, Mezreth calls it akashic. But when they break, they don't die as such. They just break apart and they splinter, but they're still there. They just change physical forms like we do.

Because that follows what Mezreth said before about life has always been here. So, you can't actually kill a life. It just transmutes and change. We as humans, some call it reincarnation, which is basically you transmute. We leave one bus, and you get in another one. While we are discussing life and death let's talk about the skulls we have seen, that's something more specific. We can get somewhere with this, surely.

This is the part that I'm interested in because if they are and they've been here and they're living here as opposed to flying past and watching and occasionally popping in but living with us. What were their intentions and dispositions. And did they use humans or liaise with them? Because that to me is the crucial element in our evolution. I hear stories of both using us sometimes as a slave race and sometimes liaising with us as equal partners. So, what was going on, and who are this mob? Where are they from, what makes them different from us and what are their motivations?

Mezreth:
Mixing and merging here, there and everywhere. We've been together for a long time, so long that the idea of ours and yours has lost meaning. We have lost meaning. There are ancient human remains dotted around the cosmos posing equal mysteries. You and they, and we – ours, yours and theirs, all meaningless – all is the same. Origin is the same for all beings.

Steve:

So it's not really part of what this planet is about why we're here and why they're here that is the essential issue. This is supposed to be a place where they're trying to merge everything into one, aren't they? All the differences merge into a common goal. And therefore, if you start talking and identifying that I come from here or there, then there's division, isn't there?

Let's dig deeper even though I'm probably going to get a cryptic response on the next question that stems off this. But primarily they are here. And when we think about the fact, like I've been trying to say when you look at the variations in humans, it's just unbelievably different. There are so many diverse genes in this equation. Clearly, they came from all over the Cosmos to live with us. They shared their genes and that's inside us now.

So now I'm going to talk about the no-forehead beings I've seen, and I have the bones of one individual. Where did these bones come from? What are their intentions?

Mezreth:

They were our siblings. Our younger kin. They left the cradle, their home, to travel for the love of curiosity. Then they made friends on and on they would go, but after ages, friendships broken and alliances took over, our little siblings got too involved and lost heart after some time, they abandoned their goals and returned home, never wanting to return again and never wanting to leave again.

Steve:

So, these are younger siblings of Mezreth and they left the cradle. When they went around from place to place, they were only doing this for the right reasons. There was no interest in making a political alliance or crusade. They walked away from the politics of that. Now, with the foreheadless race, are they still keeping to themselves?

(Lea adding context):

Yes, they're still alive, but they're not interested in anything at the moment. Well, I mean, not that they say they're not interested. They're just keeping out of it. A lot of politics out there as well. Don't worry. They're keeping out of it.

Steve:
While we're going down this path, I wanted to try something fairly pragmatic. The last question got close, so we'll try again. We're talking about different races of aliens. And really, it's funny that in this planet, nearly all the talk, apart from Pleiadians and Sirians, seems to be fixated on two groups.

And for a lot of different reasons, which we won't go into right now, I'm not sure that it's completely right, I was wondering if we could have a little bit of detail on the prime suspects in this group, which would probably be the Reptilians and Draconians. What is their take on these two groups, what they're on about and with the current state of play with them. And the consensus is they are in league with the devil and that they're completely evil. But I'm not sure that's right. But let's find out what you got for me.

Mezreth:
We represent only some of the factions. Your closest neighbours, the Xannians, they see, they fear you as you are now. But the needs on why they choose to risk themselves may frighten you in the beginning in essence, their motivations on befriending you are of survival, but you would gain much from that relationship should you master your fear. All they want is an exchange.

(Lea adding context on reptilians):
Because they have alien goals but then there are others from other factions that who are also happened to be reptilian, who have different ideas, goals and motivations. But you have to remember, it is so much easier to hate and fear a species that looks very different to you. Afterall, true evil lies in a beautiful temple wearing a pretty face.

Steve:

Exactly. Which is where I think David Icke hasn't picked up the nuances correctly in this one. He's put the Reptilians into a completely depraved group as such. And what you're telling me is that no race either here or anywhere else has a mortgage on having one opinion. It's the different ways everyone approaches it. So the great majority of Reptilians obviously fit into the hostile stereotype, but he's working with groups that don't, but they may not have exactly the same reasons for doing it, but they have a general shared goal of being and doing something good, wouldn't they?

And of course, when it comes to the Reptilians, you've got the issue where the way they're portrayed is nearly the same way the Devils is portrayed. He talks about the Reptilians because as a group, let's be honest, at least one group behaved badly and there's nothing that can get around that.

As fot that group of reptiles, there's a lot to be feared from them. But what's really important, I think Mezreth is saying this too, is that if you're going to dislike them, be careful because most might be like that, but don't make a general statement because there's going to be exceptions.

I've got one more question that follows. It looks like a huge paragraph at the moment. As mentioned before, there's an imminent change in everything just ahead. This might finish very quickly as I think my question might be longer than the answer given, I referred to this change and asked for a few words of wisdom and encouragement.

That's what I asked for before. And what happened was he indirectly passed that task back to me. He did say earlier that in the immediate times it would be ugly and brutal, and times will be distressing. If you could give just one truth, one mantra or clue to help people struggling under the oppression that could soften the blow.

My thinking is this at the moment the world has never been more preoccupied and possessed with fear. And it basically sucks the life out of people. And I know many people who are just falling underneath it because it's insidious in its grip. It's now become every part of our thinking. People are judged by issues around the damage and grief fear creates, and it's turning people against people.

I would really appreciate a practical response and I don't know what the answer is going to be, but anyway, we're going to try anyway. What is your response to my plea for something?

(Lea adding context):
This man's wrath is all about personal growth. You take the path that is the hardest and the dirtiest to trudge through, but the reward is even greater. So, if it's a path of least resistance, and something that you're comfortable with, not only do you not gain anything, but you also stand to lose something. That's not the word for word answer he gave but is close. I'm just giving you an idea of how he thinks.

Mezreth:
This time. This will defeat you, but you will not die. When these days pass, you will marvel at a strength you never knew you had then and only then will you know. You will know those days were a gift.

Steve:
I wouldn't argue with that because that's like arguing with yourself. You don't win either way. And recently I have met many who are overwhelmed by tales of fear and woe, it is becoming so dreadful. They keep returning to the sickening realty of today asking, why is evil on this planet?

And the indigenous response would be, thank God it is. Otherwise, where's the point? Without the struggle where's the point for living? If you're going to be on holidays all the time and come and look at a pretty place and come back and reply nothing at all when asked, what did you learn? You got to fight for progression it is not a free ride. So that's really important. What he's saying is the greater the battle you go through the greater the reward and there's no one on this planet who is going to escape this one.

What our Original Elders have told us is that when the change begins to take hold the birds will start to lose their lines of alignments and they won't know where they're flying, and the whales will lose their alignment too. And this will become accentuated, and it'll be the last sign. So, we know that's going to happen just not exactly when.

And I suppose what he's saying primarily is if you get through this, you'll look back and thank that you were forced to live in what's a miserable predicament, yet still live through this ascension and remain here.

Because when I go outside, I see animals, no cars, and I look at the birds, I live in a rainforest, people in the cities go out and they see and feel the concrete and negativity. Mezreth is saying at the end of it all, you can look back and smile and say, I got through this. The greater the test, the more you're going to learn. Well, this is going to be an encyclopaedic lesson. Because every day is going to be more difficult, and people are going to be turning on each other.

And I want to make one point about that. I don't really care what side you're on, whether you're going to take a needle or not take a needle or belong to any denomination. I'm not passing judgment on that. And I've got no right to pass judgment on whatever you decide is right for you. That's your decision. And I'm sure Mezreth would say the same about this.

Yeah, but don't impose that decision on another soul. Don't look down on someone because they did something you don't agree with, because when you do that, it doesn't matter what the cause, the means is never justified. The ends can't do it. It's the way you get there. If you do something where you say, that person is wrong it is you who are in error. And people are doing that in saying I hate that person, then they should be like us. You have actually fallen down. I don't care what side it comes from. Other people who don't take the vaccine talk about the people who do in the same ways, the ones who do, talk about the ones that don't. And that is a disease that goes past the vaccine and into the soul.

It goes past the vile and that's what Mezreth's talking about. So, yes, he's right in that respect. And it is a great guidance given. In other words, embrace it and then you'll overcome it. But if you fight this or that, you become part of the collateral damage.

(Lea adding commentary):
But yeah, remember, it's one of those sorts of things like it's important to embrace the lower aspects of yourself. You know, that's what this time is about. It's flinging it back into our faces. The thing is that we've all got the monster inside us that we've tried to ignore. Even people who self-proclaim themselves to be the purest and the cleanest and the highest are deluded.

Steve:
I would say that from my point of view, I think I am around a 50/50 chance of ascending and being part of this. And I think it's really important that you do embrace the monster within.

The trick is in doing so you must never fear it, but understand that every being on this planet lives in a duality of good and evil, inside and outside. And at the moment this is a reset, it's a rebalancing because we've got out of sync, and we were always going to do that. And I'm afraid Lucifer is going to have to take a back seat for a while.

But the good news is evil will not disappears from the scene. Because if it did, there would be no challenges to overcome, injustices to battle and no point in reincarnating. So, right now, my suggestion is true if you take on the philosophy of whatever when bad news or bad deeds are afoot, you will not get angry or resentful, just be.

The golden rule is don't pass judgment on another person. There's more stupidity and oppression ahead that's guaranteed, and you ought to remember if people say things that offend let it go. It serves no purpose or joy to wallow in bad news and inclination.

The drama associated with Covid is just another challenge and fork in the road, from Mezreth's perspective it is a blessing in 'sorting the wheat from the chaff.'.

(Lea adding commentary):
Well, Mezreth calls it a gift. It's a present.

Steve:
And that's what we'll call it from now on, that takes the negativity out of the wrapping. So when we refer to it, we're never going to get anywhere near the truth and opportunities until we call this the gift. . It's a gift for all of us, and it's for us to embrace or to fight.

Lea have you got anything else you wanted to add to that that he said before we finish up?

(Lea adding commentary from Mezreth):
Whatever we experience on the internal, everything outside is merely a reflection of the internal, the chaos that we are witnessing on the external all is merely a reflection, of the billions of individual minds experiencing that same havoc and the reason as to why all of this is s happening. But I think the reason why there's so much chaos is because the distractions are now gone.

And that is something that he's really emphasized that this is a time for introspection even when the distractions multiply. It's all finally surfaced, all the things that you've managed to suppress, all the things that you've tried and managed to avoid are now returning because they've never really been properly managed. No-one has been properly mapped. Not one living being on this planet has totally managed a way of dealing with their internal demons.

And I think this is a time is needed in order to save the world in so many ways. I don't like using that sort of dramatic language, but the only way we can do that is if we can solve what's going on inside. And that is something that he's really put a lot of time and effort into emphasizing with me.

I remember this from years and years of having contact with him, he doesn't like to sugar-coat things for me. Essentially, he said you are of no use to anyone if you can't solve yourself first. You can't do anything if you can't solve yourself first.

Steve:

So, what Mezreth is talking about now is all of this chaos that we're seeing on the surface is merely a reflection of what's going on within each of us. It's bringing all this to the surface and the Original saying of as on top, so below is now becoming 'our daily bread.' It is happening in an area where you don't have to look up that high or low, it's all over the place. On top of that other things will be thrown into the mix and they are all part of what we're creating in ourselves. The power and passion within us is spreading across the planet.

Transcript Four

Steve:

I asked about the beginning of life from the Big Bang then everything that followed after, to which he said, life has always been here. Maybe the Big Bang is no more than life creating matter as a place of residence to give purpose and a way to test and measure each soul's progress.

Mezreth:

The Big Bang was a point of change, but life existed before. Like the many other cataclysms before, when life decided to change. We can still see the waves of the big bang rippling out in the black and its many predecessors. Life changes. It's a must for the universal stagnates and its consciousness falters. Don't fear death of life as you know it. Fear the death of challenge.

Steve:

In other words, what he is saying is that cataclysms and changes are here for that reason, isn't it? It's a challenge. But that could change again.

(Lea adding commentary):

It has to and it comes in waves. So, it's always slightly different each time, but every wave of change that comes is not beyond those who are experienced to overcome it. That's something that has to be remembered. It's not like, you come to this point of no return in declaring you can't do anything about it. Problems come paired with solutions, so it does take time.

Steve:

All right. So that's what matter is for, it's a way of creating challenges. And, of course, with every challenge, there's an option within that. On a slightly different tangent I asked Mezreth about

146

God, after all God is the sole agent involved in bringing the Big Bang into existence. He said it was regarded differently in different manifestations, pure equality, intelligence and of course with human features in some cases.

Taking one step backward what of the supposed opposite force to God? There has always been a manifestation in the opposite side to this Divine equation which has often been referred to as Satan or Lucifer. So, the question of what is or was Lucifer is ever-present. I wanted to ask about this.

Is this an opposing energy or force? And, has Lucifer always existed, or is it a collective figment of some people's imagination? And what about this notion of the fallen angel? Is that Lucifer's fate? So, I want to get my head around what is this being that's supposed to be the Supreme Lord of Evil? What's he got to say in that regard?

Mezreth:
You figure it out. Akashi is God, Akashi is Lucifer. Akashi is the same across. It's me and you. Akashi is pull and push inside and outside. Akashi is stupid and intellectual as it is war and peace. There's no opposite to the All as there is no name for non-existence.

Steve:
What he's saying is that it's all the same. Two sides of the same coin. So, it is given a name and an entity. Lucifer exists but only as a creation of us. That would mean the concept of Lucifer or the Devil is a construct people are making to sort of excuse their way of avoiding faults and nuances by saying, the Archons made me do it. What they're really saying is, I wouldn't normally do this, but I did this time.

Well, then the next question becomes superfluous to an extent, but we'll go with it anyway because it'll probably turn into something unexpected. Now, is this force or being Lucifer, purely evil without compassion, or perhaps it is a guardian who's ordained to test and assess the merit and fortitude of each incarnated soul? In asking this I sort of know the answer because he told us before that they're both the same side of us.

Mezreth:
We are flawed because there would be no other reason to continue. Distractions are also a test for you given by you. The ones who fall behind, who do damage are children. Nothing more or less. They should not be praised or pitied. You know how long that path will be. And it will take many years or lifetimes for them to see but wish them well on the journey that all of us had to take.

Steve:
That's about what I thought, too. So that really means this is just part of the journey and this construct reminds me of scenes from a TV series called Lucifer. He is still the son of God throughout his fall and redemption. And he's actually part of the same Creator to begin with. So this is a construct we've created as a convenient way to excuse our faults and insecurities.

Question number four, a question where I think I already know the answer. Back to our Creator and the designs and tests. There are three beliefs on this planet in regard to what happens when the body dies, nothing at all, we spend eternity after one life in the immortal plane of Heaven or Hell or reincarnating since the beginning. But only one of them can be right. I feel like this is going to be very straightforward, an easy answer to predict-which is a very rare event when talking to Mezreth. Then the question is which of the three options is right?

Mezreth:
Justice. If you want to master content, you will. If you wish, splendour and joy, you will. If you wish damnation because you feel deserved, you will. If you wish to return to the canvas, you will not.

Steve:

All I can get is a basic take on this. Sounds to me like each soul chooses, if you believe nothing you get nothing, so too if convinced it is just one life on-world, so be it. But if you either believe in, or embrace once knowing it is your call, that reincarnation is the way to go, then that's where you go, again and again. Outside that thumbnail sketch I'm just going to pass on adding more. Lea made a comment that deeply resonated with me in relation to the inner battle being a constant issue for every soul breathing. Whereas she said some try to manage their demons while others hide them, and that those who deceive themselves must bear the consequences.

Mezreth:

Management of demon thoughts are here for that. Again, management of demons is the key to unlock the higher doors of existence. Sometimes it's tricky to figure out which ones need management, since they shapeshift into other issues that need attention. Sadly, the ones that cause the most grief and shame is why so few are willing to face them. But remember, those feelings are their way of deterring you from your self-mastery.

Steve:

It seems Lea was correct, as self-mastery begins with knowing all aspects of self, and since every soul incarnated has demons to face that never maintain a constant identity, denying their existence is denying part of who each person is. If you hide something, then you don't confront it and the longer that continues, the deeper the pit. People who feel they are fully ascended are deceiving themselves.

And the fact that concern me and, in particular directly concerns such people who proclaim some sort of Divine Dispensation, is that if they look very carefully, they might be shocked to find their demons have transformed into something completely different.

Let's hone in on one aspect of this denial. We use the word demons before as if they have taken up an internal residence inside all seven billion souls living on this planet.

I wanted to go further here in asking, what are demons? And they're opposites, are they angels? Or, are these angels Aliens, or are they mystical beings of an ethereal constitution? What are these things/entities within he talked about?

Mezreth:
Demons and angels are figments of your mind's way of trying to understand itself. Such as untold scores of souls, figments of Akashi trying to understand itself. If you speak intent, they are intangible terms. Our presence has been thoroughly documented there and you assume that's to certain roles long before you understood who we are.

(Lea adding context):
I'd like to focus on the first and the okay, so the first half of question six, that demons and angels are figments of your mind's eye trying to externalise itself, such as untold scores of souls are figments of Akashi trying to understand itself. Basically, what we are projecting is on a really macro scale.

We are simply everything that we see, everything that we perceive, we express all of our more complicated traits and different shades of ourselves onto different things, and then allocate some categories to them. We have to express it on the outside.

That's kind of a form of projection, the externalised cues take a familiar scare-goat in visualising our way of being able to identify what we're thinking and feeling.

Steve:
Oh, I see, it's all about self-projection. When we talk about demons and angels and we see a demon or an angel and we claim we've seen something, we're actually looking at ourselves.

(Lea adding commentary):
Well, our association with those things. Now when you're talking strictly about demons and angels actually being things. It is a metaphor documenting your faults and insecurities.

Steve:
And in other words, it's a bit like this, the Original people and we've heard Original Elder, Trudy Roberts speaks about this before, all use the words Sky Hero. The same way in our society, we use the word angel, the Original people call them Sky Heroes. These are people who come from the sky and from many other constellations, beings who come from the sky and who are regarded by humans as heroes, who can help us. To some people that sounds a lot like angels

And they didn't allocate motives and intentions by calling call them angels or demons as such, did they? They talk about spirits, and we get to decide whether they are good or bad.

Now I want to personalise this journey into the stars and the beginning in asking a question that relates to him alone. Do you regret coming or being posted here? Because I don't know which it is, to be honest. And where is your home planet?

Mezreth:
I was born in vacuum. You were born on stone. Where the vacuum and stone is not relevant. Since we are born here in this universe, I have no regrets in my coming here, but I'm not void of regrets.

Steve:
He doesn't have like the Original people do, that strong connection with a certain piece of land which they are bound by and worship. That's not in his thinking.

(Lea adding context):
Well, you have to also remember Mezreth and his kin have been around for a very, very long time. They lost the need to be tangible

and physical in the way we are. They don't need to live on any rock to physically sustain themselves.

They have been so far removed from physicality that they can live indefinitely in a vacuum for however long they want. But the point is they don't have the same limitations or vulnerabilities as we do, because they're so old and they've been around for so long. They just travel all around everywhere they go, every path, every star, every galaxy and every solar system is part of their home-base. The universe is as much their house as it is for our four walls.

Steve:
Remaining on this theme of present residence irrespective of whether it's everywhere or one locality. I wanted to find out if what many claim, including Lea, is true. Where there times in the past when aliens and humans lived together on this planet? And if so, why did this arrangement stop?

Mezreth:
In times of Atlantis, we were together, and even before that. All peoples in the interstellar community were too young to appreciate each other. So, they returned to their cradles to grow a little more. Lots of lanterns. I was already lost for the moon guardians lost themselves.

(Lea adding context):
There was a lot of contact between multiple different civilizations, even during the times of Atlantis. There wasn't just humans and one other species. It was many different religions. We were all in this sort of interstellar community with multiple different races. And around roughly the same time, there was a major issue.

Atlantis fell apart because of many political problems and other things, and of course, some very sinister rings. But the other groups, the other races also had their own problems that they were also fighting with, with their own issues.

So, it wasn't just humans, it was happening all over the Cosmos. But he says it from an outsider's perspective. He's saying that you guys lost touch with yourselves and each other and so did many Aliens. All of us were either willingly or unwillingly pushed apart and had to go back home to their cradle to grow a little more.

Steve:
What he's saying is it was more like something that had repercussions everywhere.

(Lea adding context):
What happened here was a microcosm of what was going on everywhere else. It's just that Lemuria and Atlantis were of far greater significance to us. One of those Alien groups, the Ezoni, lost their own civilization, their own cities are far more advanced and refined, and that was a big deal to them, as Atlantis is to us.

Steve:
So that's probably why that fundamental piece of history has been so cleverly hidden and turned into myths and allegories written by Plato, Pliny the Elder and Homer. But this fall from grace was all part of something bigger as some of the other races also had their demons to do deal with also and had to go back and sort them out. And that's what we've still been doing ever since.

(Lea adding context):
We're still living in Atlantis' shadow. We never really left or resolved, but basically staggered forward. So, we're still sort of reeling from that. The others are still also suffering the consequences. But the difference is, that there's been an acknowledgment and the honouring of truth in some of the other off-world locations. We did the normal response of avoiding the problem and hoped it would go away. But not all, some are still reeling from their own losses and issues. Until a resolution and balance is met, they will never be free and nor will we.

None of us are free of the human condition and the human condition is not just exclusive to humans. It's everywhere. It's on all sides. Mezreth said "my regrets are void in my coming here, but I'm not void of regrets." He is a super being who can do almost anything, yet he has regrets. Regrets about what?

Steve:
I would have to assume that as wise as he is, he still makes mistakes. Otherwise, there would be no point being here.

During these times of chaos, suspicion and fear why didn't some of the aliens who were not subjected to this imbalance come down and offer assistance or guidance. Why didn't they come down and say boys and girls this is what we should do?

Mezreth:
We are. We're doing it now, as we've always done. We won't burst into the bedroom while a child wields a gun. It's a recipe for further heartache. I've seen the consequences before. If you want us to do more, you must reach us halfway.

Steve:
In other words, there they are doing just that but not overtly. But we've got to make the steps and ask them. The problem is at the moment, officially, Aliens and UFOs still don't even exist.

Now let's look deeper into the psyche of these earthly inhabitants only this time instead of probing into our faults and deficiencies, what of the positives? What quality do humans have that you find most appealing and inspiring, and what qualities do they also possess that you find most disappointing?

Mezreth:
Humans create innovative ways to cheat the test.

Steve:

I expected a touch more than eight words, but it actually says everything. So we are all about creating innovative ways to cheat the test.

(Lea adding context):

And he's indirectly also saying that he admires the innovation of those of us who are able to problem solve through admitting that we actually acknowledge our inner demons. But the negative aspect is constantly trying to cut corners, trying to take the easier path of least resistance, which again leads to nothing but further problems down the line.

Steve: What he admires is that while we cheat many tests, he loves the creativity employed in avoiding the truth. Actually, that negativity sort of resonates with me because when I look at humans, there's a lot to look at and shake your head and say, 'Why am I part of this?' But there's two redeeming achievements I've always seen in humanity that inspire me the most. And its art and music, because it is pure creativity of the highest order, it is the purest and most elemental process in creating something out of nothing. An artist begins the process with a blank sheet of paper or canvas, and a musician has an instrument, his or her fingers and nothing else. Lea, I know you've mentioned to me before there's one alien race that has a type of ambient music you really like that you claim is better than all music on Earth. I think it is somewhat like the music of Tangerine Dream and Mike Oldfield.

And I get that, but I don't believe there's any planet anywhere that can have such a variety type of music which includes rock, progressive rock, reggae, pop, country and western, along with every style of music imaginable and some that you couldn't. But then again, with Mezreth in the room, I could be wrong again. And, of course, the same diversity applies with art. We seem to be possessed with this massive amount of creativity, alas not always aided by a great deal of intellect to actually complement this process, but the potential and huge creativity is inherent.

But that does seem to be a strength that we have the creativity to be able to look at things in new ways, maybe surprise everyone. I think if it exists in art music and then it could spread into other areas.

I've got one more question left to ask and to me in some respects, this is the one we're focused on the most. Ten years from now, could you briefly, briefly describe what that would look like on the planet Earth and those humans allowed to remain?

Mezreth:
A new set of problems but you won't be able to solve them without moulding the tools from your current issues. Don't worry about tomorrow.

Steve:
We won't be utterly void of problems. There's still going to be problems at every point, at every stage or level, and every progression of one's life. To assume that there's going to be this utopian society that is utterly free, where everyone's peaceful and happy, which will be served up on a platter is a mistake as nothing comes for free. Even then there will still be problems, but I suspect the solutions will be easier to find and act upon.

(Lea adding commentary):
If you experience one emotion for too long, you kind of forget what the other ones feel like. Even with joy and happiness that can become neglected and devalued if that's all there is, it still has to be earnt.

Don't worry about the possibilities of what tomorrow's going to look like, worry about creating and using effectively the tools to solve the situation as it is now, then plan ahead

If everything is exactly the way that they envision everything to be, there is an inherent inertia that could lead on to stagnation. And then at that point it spirals into deterioration, and Mezreth has often said his race have to constantly battle with this dead end. Because life falls apart without having any kind of resistance or challenges on a societal and individual scale. Things decay after a while, and he bore witness to this himself.

And even his mob tried to eliminate all the problems that this group was experiencing before. But what they ended up creating was a society of placid, lazy, just as selfish and self-centred beings, and they were worse than us.

Steve:

It's written in a lot of scriptures, that there will be a golden age of a thousand years where everything's perfect. And I've seen Christian literature and depictions where you've got people sitting down with a lamb and a lion and they're all patting one another.

That's not going to happen. We're not going to have a thousand years of golden evil-free existence where everyone smiles at each other, and no-one is challenged or called to task. But I suppose when you think about it, there's not one person on this planet that's perfect. There'll be a mixture of people with different strengths and weaknesses, and some people will still not like other people. There still will be things said about other people they won't like. If that didn't happen, if there was nothing that was disruptive or upsetting, then there would be nothing for us to learn.

Mezreth:

We are flawed because there would be no reason to continue this.

Steve:

If we're all angels on Earth sitting around on a cloud, looking at each other, smiling at each other. And the content of the conversations would be, "Oh I know that," "I agree," "I was thinking the same thing." Everyone would be saying and thinking the same things, and no-one would ever problem solve, and if that came to pass, life would become miserable.

So, in one respect, and I think he made this point before today, what's happening right now and the perceived injustices which are so many is a gift. He didn't say it was a curse, he said it was a gift.

Because those are the challenges and insults that bring out the best and worst in us, and therefore, that gives you a real and present chance to deal with your demons. Some people do and some don't, and I've noticed that what's interesting is that it doesn't matter which political or social side of the fence you are positioned on. I don't know what the political terms left and right means anymore.

I think that stance changes from issue to issue. But the one common reaction that is happening right now is that everyone seems to be experiencing inner turmoil and is forced to make a decision.

(Lea adding commentary):
What I gather from the main theme of this was the introspection, the internal universe takes precedence over the external. This growth has always been about the teachings he's given to me and the things we've often talked about.

He almost discounts the external universe. What's inside you and what's inside me? What's in here? That's the only universe that he actually cares about.

Steve:
He's really interested in so below and sees on top as basically an external setting that really doesn't count for anything. It's just a place to reside within.

And then what happens within you is the universe. And within both universes I know that our guides from above are very happy about the fact there was a successful ceremony at Uluru. But he also made it very clear there is no guarantee because it's successful that we are all going to be part of this. So, the question is, does he think we will make it? Is there some sort of hope at the end of this tunnel? Because a lot of it's pretty dire at the moment.

(Lea adding commentary):
That's an interesting question because I've often questioned that myself, not just for myself, but for the whole. What one part of me says he's been doing this for so long and he's actually tallied up a list of successes as well as failures, and he has ample time and resources.

Considering the fact that he has such a long connection with this place, but he's also had lives here as well. He actually cares more about this place than I do.

Steve:
So, he has an emotional investment in this place, hasn't he?

(Lea adding commentary):
Yeah. And I can't see him not putting in not only just time and energy, but himself. He's pouring himself here and his patience is unreal. His patience is supernatural, almost because of his status. You know, it transcends what any of us of the physical plane possess.

Steve:
That's what I was trying to get out of these questions.

Transcript Five

Steve:

I wanted to focus on one theory, one aspect, which is the existence of Heaven and Hell. Why? Because it's the focal issue of concern for every being on this planet that dies. If we understood why we are here and what happens after the physical body dies, this life would be a lot easier. So, let's have a go. No guarantee we'll get any right answers.

The first question I wrote is related to the popular notion of hell is a lack of a location. But is that true? After completing a ceremony recently with one of the rings from Atlantis, and I'm not going to go into the details, there are two lines from a song that resonated with me. By the way, I don't have any INXS albums.

There is one song that has the words, 'the devil inside, the devil inside, every single one of us has the devil inside." Is the lyricist, right? So that's the first question. If so, how do we deal with this demon in residence? Is it best to fight, flight or manage?

Mezreth:

Heaven and hell are not separate planes, nor are they on Earth. They live within you. You're your own angels and demons. Any good or misfortune that befalls you is sometimes out of one's control. But what is your ability to handle it. If you run from your demons, they grow larger. If you fight them, then you become them. But if you master yourself, then you are king.

Steve:

Actually, that's the first time in quite some time I can honestly say that's about what I expected. By the way, that's only after asking other questions which changed my understanding anyway. I like the last part of that which talks about fight, flight and manage. I think that was really clever.

If you fight your fails, they become you. That's exactly right. It's funny how people think when approaching adversity, I know this is a bit of a diversion, but it does fit in. There was a campaign raising money for some form of cancer, and they hired a shop, and they had pictures of toilets and an actual toilet, which had a plaque above it stating, Let's flush cancer down the toilet.

So, let's attack it. Let's fight it. And I kept thinking to myself, after my wife went through the cancer, she had embraced it. And it's when you embrace something, you no longer fight it. You don't run from it. You don't fight it. You then get to understand it.

And of course, that does lead onto some questions. When people talk about the fact that you go up to heaven and down for hell, that's their internal location. It's all in here, isn't it? So, the INXS quote is valid, which it obviously is, so does the reverse reply in relation to what is termed Heaven? We sort of answered this before, but any clarification or extension will assist. Other people who have died return describing different scenes and setting. Is that a place of internal construct or actual location.

Mezreth:
What you experience in your afterlife, is only for you to know. I don't know for certain what you'll see and feel, but if you know you're alive, then you will know more than I.

Steve:
You create your heaven and hell. If you've done a lot of bad things, once departing from here you go over and over the pain and distress each mistake creates. It's very much like that line in the TV show we mentioned earlier called Lucifer. He says that hell has no doors that are closed. I think it's a beautiful line. So, in other words, you create the prison walls and time of penance. You could walk in that door and you could walk out the door.

We got that. Now, that being the case, here is an issue that I'm interested in, and that's why I asked the first two questions to lay down the foundations of my personal interest and to an extent, yours. When this topic was last raised, Mezreth spoke of one supreme entity, there was no division.

If so, what is Lucifer or Satan? Is this purely an internal manifestation or an interlocutor and manager of negative energies and co-author of the exam you spoke of that humans can't creatively avoid or suspend? My question is, what is this concept that we have of Lucifer and Satan? Is it our own head creating it, or is there a spirit of some form that is an organizer?

Mezreth:
Lucifer is a symbol, a category for you to better understand the fluidity of existence. Like all other divine entities, they are representatives of virtues for you to choose, to adapt or discard. The power of choice is frightening, but it is your fundamental right.

Steve:
Now we've got something we can talk about. Lucifer is a symbolic statement of each soul's cause and effect. It's an expression of the divine entity and a personification juxtaposed against my foibles and failings.

(Lea adding context):
As humans, we tend to box and categorize certain things. What is good, what is bad, what is mischievous, what is benevolent, and so our vices continue. He looks at things as equal things right across the plane. He doesn't look at good. He doesn't see good. He doesn't see evil. He sees these traits within all of us, within all beings. Our understanding of divine entities is basically copying us to express this. So, when he says Lucifer is an aspect or direction of the divine, or that Archangel Gabriel is divine, that it's the same to him. Therefore, it's all divine.

Steve:
He doesn't pass a value judgment on what we do and how we do things-he expects both. They're all different ways of tilting the light.

Out of the greatest evil can come a greater good. Everything's a matter of choice, isn't it?

Lucifer is not actually like the character in the TV show, he is actually me and you. The version that's of slightly shaved face standing about six foot five with glimpses of red eyes at any given moment is the actor's devil incarnate. There is not a being or an interlocutor that is actually Satan. It's a creation we've made that gives our impulses some personal space and 'elbow room.'.

With the devil given its rightful position that brings us back to the exam Mezreth said we so cleverly avoid , of which humans found excuses and distractions. In a nutshell, what is the content and curriculum of this exam?

What is this exam that we are so cleverly able to avoid?

Mezreth:
You make the right choice. The exam is to see if you are going to make the right choice. Every one of those choices are bought with consequences. You've always been at the crossroads, but now those crossroads cannot be ignored or left until later. Apathy won't save you.

Steve:
And there's something really important in that we have always had this this ability or inability to make the right choice. But he made the point that right now we are at the crossroads. So this time around what we did before that necessitated us returning to the Earth classroom isn't going to work, is it? We have to make a final decision. This time we have to make a choice and bear the consequences.

But this time, it's not that easy. As for making choices, isn't that what we do every minute of every day? I mean, every time we walk forward, we have a choice to go forward, backward, to the side or stop. Which way do we put our next foot? And up until now, you can make mistakes and try again, but not now.

Let's look outside ourselves and take some time to consider another factor in the Alien equation of which there are so many to choose from. Was there ever a species of reptilians living on this planet either before or during the time of hominids? It is a constant topic of conversation and I feel some clarity is needed here. Do these reviled reptilians actually exist? And if so, what was and maybe still is, their general opinion of Homo sapiens?

Mezreth:
There's been many species on and around earth, like many other worlds. It's not unique. There's a long history with humans and Zanashj, but Zanashj are not reptilian, though their appearance can trick the inexperienced eye. They were shapeshifters taking faces of many to adapt to many environments. They made poor choices, but now seek redemption from those they have damaged. Some are here now, learning from the same school as you.

Steve:
So we didn't get an answer on Reptilians as such, but we did get an answer on Zanashj, which might turn out to be an indirect yes. It would seem Reptilians are actually shapeshifters. And so where does that put David Icke in all of this? Because he spent his whole career following and reviling Reptilians and saying that they're still here.

(Lea adding context):
Yes. It's not a very good history, but just because Zanashj had this very deep pocket of unpleasant history, they have actually changed because he does say that they are back, they are trying, but some of them are actually trying to seek that redemption. They are trying to do something more than what their ancestors did and what many of us still do as well. They want more than just a string of failures and abuse.

Some are indifferent, some just simply don't care and some do. I can't speak about for the entire species because I don't know them. But I do know that a few are actually invested in trying to seek out redemption. And some of them are coming here and helping us out because they know that they've messed around with us at some points in history. And they know that a lot of the events that happen post their interventions and interferences are their fault. If they didn't behave so badly on Earth, we may not be in the state that we are right now.

Steve:
They sort of do fit into that reptilian mould that we've given them, but we've done that basically because we've looked at them like I did. I can superficially see the reptilian side in there. That's just their physical features and that means very little.

I'm looking at the next question and I sort of asked this before, but I'll read it out, because I was really trying to chase this up from so many different angles. Some have theorized the inspiration behind the concept of the devil incarnate on this planet is a reptilian leader spirit full and vengeance. Is the concept of a devil a fictional account used to make the flock fearful?

Mezreth:
Stories change and shift from the bias, from the biased mouths of the teller and the biased ears of the listener, those that are not physically repulsive if they do not wish it so. Their actions, however, were so they were depicted as such. Those that were never pure evil. If evil did have a face, it would be one of beauty and innocence. You and they have a lot in common. You and they have a lot of common ground.

Steve:
You're referring to. Who, us?

Mezreth:
Yes. Collectively.

Steve:

We got a lot of exactly what we were looking for. We are our demons and devils, and they are us.

. With Lucifer being a human construct and excuse, we do need to examine our motives and intentions. The human condition is an enigmatic and contradictory piece of work. All nonhuman, earthly species seem to have a general set of ways of behaving and interacting. Humans can be serial killers, philosophers, pacifists and mercenaries. We can be Hitler, Stalin, Tesla, Ghandi, Plato and Martin Luther King.

Why are we so unpredictable because all other animals on this planet have general traits of behaviour, and they are fairly predictable. You cannot predict any human on this planet, why is that?

Mezreth:

The human condition is not exclusive to humans. No one will ever be free from it. The difference is we devoted more time to communication and understanding of each individual, what their strengths and weaknesses are. We know why someone is the way they are. We know why they have made their choices. And we try to facilitate environments where they flourish. They are like seeds, but no two seeds are alike.

Steve:

That probably sums it up really well. You think about humans, and you say to yourself, which face is the same and you don't have an answer. Which fingerprints are the same? You don't have an answer. But I suppose that just fits in with everything else. With humans they can weigh 40 kilos or 400 kilos, some stand half a metre tall and others h two and a half metres. They really do, at a physical level, have nothing in common with each other. Mezreth did say before that the outside is a reflection of the inside. Well, if we're all completely different then we can be everything, can't we? So, it's not a human condition, it's just a condition.

(Lea adding commentary):
No, the human condition is not exclusive to humans. Everyone has it and no one will ever be free from it. It's just how you control it, how you master it, or how you do not control it because it doesn't really care for control. It's about the being the master of self. But what you can do is to master yourself and once you have achieved that, everything else outside of you falls back into place.

Steve:
What that also means is that some of the people who follow the alien story and believe in it, place these aliens on pedestals as being all knowing, all good or perfect. That would be as naive as placing a human on a pedestal. Let's just deviate slightly from Aliens who have fallen to those who have ascended. What about Mezreth's race? Are they all-knowing and good? Or are there variations within?

(Lea adding commentary):
There are variations absolutely, but there are no absolutes in this universe. First of all, however, from what I have observed in my communications with all others, Mezreth's mob seems to be the most uniform. However, he does speak about some of the others, like they have their different names. They have different characteristics. Different traits, but for me they all kind of roughly look the same. But they have their own different vibes. They all have their different energies, and they invoke different things in whomever they are exposed to. So no, they may look somewhat similar but they're not all the same.

Steve:
There are a whole lot of variations within and without.

(Lea adding context):
So, basically what people have got to get used to is that we're all the same but in completely different ways.

Steve:
Mezreth did say that we are at the crossroads at this time, and that we've got to make a decision. So it does follow from that question. Why is it so important right now for each person to choose? Is it to balance their books, make amends and control their demons is that because there is an exam ahead that no one can cheat or avoid? And if so, what is the mark if you have score to earn the right to stay?

Mezreth:
If you have correctly nurtured a person, you have saved the world. The exam is your life, and the results are the lives that come after. The only failure is the one where you repeat the same mistakes in the assumption that you will pass. For now, the passing grade is to avoid making that same mistake in this century.

Steve:
In this century, that just confirms the fact that this is the final countdown. You've got to get it right now. The way to pass this exam is to not make the same mistakes you've made that got you here.

This is not an easy exam and don't think it's merely matter of turning up and saying the right things and thinking nice thoughts, that's not enough.

It's more than that. I've got to tell you. You have to deal with yourself without fear or favour. And that's really tough.

You've got to own up to your sins and indiscretions too. That might be hard for some people, knowing that this interaction has been going on for so long with so many different alien species involved, has there ever been conflict or serious disagreement between them? And if so, how has this been resolved? And having you telling me that they're no different to us, I have to assume that they must have had conflict. How did they get around that?

Mezreth:

The Zanashj have been humbled by their arrogance, their assumption that they sat at the top of the pyramid in their sphere of influence, made them forgetful and small. Their weaknesses were discovered and exploited, and the dominion on many worlds shrunk until their influence caved in. Earth was also in their dominion, but you (humans,) you cast them away at the right time. Zanashj have never recovered from those days, nor do they ever intend on repeating them. Can you say the same for yourselves?

Steve:

All right, that's an interesting last comment. That's what this is all about. Can we say the same, well right now the answer obviously is no we haven't got it right at all.

Being humbled by arrogance is a good thing, but on the other side of the fence there are three rings from Atlantis that have never been humble and certainly are arrogant. I know you've heard me say many times that there's a lot of evil in Atlantis that's been a constant, hasn't it? And I know these rings have been knee-deer in the thick of it

Since we found the three rings, they have been associated with chaos, deceit, lies, sickness, curses and murder ceremonies. It's a situation they thrive in, but are the rings solely responsible due to their evil disposition? Or do they merely shake free the devil inside. Are the three rings from Atlantis a conduit that seeks out and amplifies your demons, or is there something more sinister contained within each ring?

Mezreth:

They're only tools. They maximize whatever traits you have, and the larger your ego becomes from their monstrous power, and they will only add to that vicious cycle. Those tools are also part of the exam, and the right choice is to leave them be. Atlanteans had similar tools that allowed their empire to flourish and look what happened.

Steve:
That would mean the fact that one of those three rings I've hidden from everyone and destroyed that ring. No-one knows where it is, he would be quite happy with that. What we're getting from that is, yes, they do give you access to the good and bad inside you. I've destroyed one of the three, because it was stolen then used time after time badly and was lost in bad thoughts and horrible actions.

I think it is uncontainable and dangerous to be in existence anywhere on this planet, which is why I'm the only person who knows where the remains are hidden. The other two I'm still working with and, to be honest, that doesn't give me much hope.

I had this vision. That I could get some sort of modicum of agreement and conciliatory reactions from one of the two rings still intact. But maybe this is a lost cause. That these three tools are also part of the exam, is something unexpected, and it could be that the right choice is to leave them be, or maybe not.

I'll have to think about that. Because we're not doing rings today, I won't go further down that path. That was as illuminating as it was troubling.

Transcript Six

Steve:
Duncan Roads told me of a time when his pet dog was on death's door, he contacted the best animal whisperer in the country for guidance. She began by asking him to leave the room as he was the problem. And I can tell you, Duncan was shocked because he loves that dog.

When he was allowed to return, she told him that because Duncan was trying so hard to keep the dog alive and with him, the dog couldn't cross over and was solely hanging on for him. She said the dog had a secret, and this is where it gets interesting. His dog had a sacred role on the other side in teaching dogs how to control their more basic instincts and devote themselves to teaching humans unconditional love. Was he correct?

Mezreth:
Animals are not masters or servants to any other animal, but two souls can arrange their roles for each other.

Steve:
Now that's interesting because the people who believe in reincarnation and even the people who believe in heaven and hell, have this belief that when they go to the other side, there will be other human souls that will be waiting for them. And what you're telling me there is a relationship with an animal and a human.

So that that means that there really is not this big distinction between humans and all other forms of life. I know a lot of Christian people have this belief that there is a pyramid of life, and we stand at the apex above all others. However, there are many people who have forged a strong relationship with dogs who feel this is wrong and that they could be there waiting to greet them. So, it turns out they're right.

But that relates to the second question. What follows is whether this is just dogs, or does this extend further, and if so, how far?

On this occasion I was inspired by Lea and it's to do with our last conference. And what people didn't see before we started, was that you had a cat crawling all over you. Now the cat clearly loved and cared about you. Could it be that some cats have also been given the task of teaching humans pure love?

Mezreth:
Cats and dogs express love differently from physical to a soul level, same as some humans and non-terrestrials. My expression of love is unlike to the kin beside me. What matters is that expression.

Steve:
Cats and dogs are different in their manner, in the way they behave but what binds them is that they both crave love. I saw an example of that animal love when I went to a public outdoor meeting recently and spent some time watching one dog that was actually walking around with this young child and then putting his paw forward and holding his hand. It seemed to me that dogs are very open in their displays of affection, whereas cats tend to be selective and picky about when they seek or give love. From every perspective, these animals are a mirror-reflection of what we are ourselves. They do say there are dog people and cat people …

And you start to wonder whether the cat people are more like cats. And that's what Mezreth is saying. I want to close this animal connection with a personal anecdote and musing that relates to Mezreth's insistence that the soul of any animal is no different than ours. Evans rabbit lived over thirteen years, which is exceptionally long for any rabbit. We would like to think that when we pass over, his soul will greet us. Is that just wishful thinking or the real truth?

Mezreth:
When souls depart life, they shed parts of the former personality is copied over, but what they were in life was returned to something

more balanced. Some souls wish to wait. What some souls wish is to find other fields. But if there was a strong bond to the living, then they often say I can't.

Steve:

What I find fascinating is that the animals also get to choose according to what they want, that is no different to us and makes me wonder what is the difference between humans and many sorts of life? The last three questions lead into the question I really wanted to ask, and that's why I went about this in steps. The question I find really interesting and I'm not sure how this is going to turn out, sums up the other three. Speaking of souls, is there any difference at all between dogs, cats and rabbits, and that of humans?

Mezreth:

No difference. There's no cats, no snakes, no human soul – it's totally pure. Those former states are gone, except, the only difference is the wisdom and experience gained to aid in the advancement of that self.

Steve:

I had a suspicion throughout that we are all the same, so let's go back to the dog I saw that was giving love out to everyone. And particularly when this kid was chatting and patting the dog, he had his eyes closed, his head was arched back, and he was just living in pure ecstasy bathed in love. That particular dog would be far more advanced than quite a few human beings I've met.

This belief that somehow or other our human soul sits above all other animals is a mistake that has serious consequences, in that so much of the truth about living and dying has been perverted. Wisdom is not the exclusive precinct of educated adults. I remember when I was with our three-year-old grandson. And as we were walking down a track together asked to us, is life just a dream? A logical progression of Mezreth's last comment is to ask him that if humans can incarnate as animals, then can animals incarnate as humans?

This sounds to be a very indigenous observation as there was a time when the indigenous peoples across many continents spoke about animals' souls in the same way they spoke about human souls. They did not differentiate. And I remember an Old Way Original story of a ceremony when they went to hunt, which must begin with the song and the dance that takes place before.

The men danced for over two hours, and they danced so hard and vigorously that upon finishing some actually collapsed. It was all about giving reverence and respect to the animal they intended to kill. After completing this ritual, they went out to hunt and came back empty-handed, and had clearly failed in their task. What they did is they went back to one person who they felt did not put enough energy and respect in his dance to revere convince the soul of that animal that it should give itself to the tribe.

The blame was placed upon a person who danced poorly, thus not giving enough respect. Knowing that they regarded the souls of animals to be our equal and one dance fell short of the high standard required, next time that dancer would be watched ever so closely. Enough of the two- and four-footed animals, I'd like to examine the credentials of the winged creatures. And in particular, I'm fascinated by a couple of aspects of birds that I've never fully understood and maybe Mezreth can shine a light on that.

Many assume that birds communicate solely by sound, but I've got an issue with that. How can flocks of hundreds and sometimes thousands of bird's twist and turn while in flight all at the same time in perfect synchronicity, yet never collide. You put a mob of humans clustered together and see what happens, and they'll trample and collide.

Obviously, something's going on there. What am I looking at there? What happens with these birds? Is this all through one bird's audible or visual direction, or are all birds communicating through some form of communal telepathic thought process that we don't fully understand yet?

Mezreth:

The living and dead ride the waves of the sea of consciousness. We all feel it, but not all know it. It's part of the invisible orchestra of the universe. In some places, the music is mute, while in other places, the music is full. Earth has a song, but it's a pity only few can hear it.

Steve:

So, they ride the waves of the sea of consciousness and we don't ride, nor can we hear it. Then that tells us something about where we should be flying, walking or running. And it's obvious we are not in the right place. Let's stay with the birds a little further and talk about those wild birds that are flying all over the place. If flying free, that cannot include the chooks and birds we put in cages because that kills their lifestyle, vitality and changes so many things.

Excluding the domesticated birds which do not count. I'm talking about the birds in the rainforest where we live at the moment that fly as they wish and go where they want.

We've got these birds circling freely in the sky, of which there are billions of birds on this planet at any given time. And most birds, except the parrots, don't live that long so I've got an issue with the death-count. Now this is where it gets tricky, if not killed by a predator, climatic extreme, collision or speeding cars, I've never seen a dead bird. I've been out in the bush a lot, more than most people and not once have I seen a dead bird laying anywhere.

What I've seen are thousands flying around. Now, this is an issue for me. Why aren't we need deep in feathers? How do these birds die and where are the bodies, because I can't find them, and I have been looking for clues or feathered corpses.

You hear them all the time, but they're never on the ground. I want to know where they go when they die because I'm not finding them anywhere. This is a different type of question, and for the first time I am not sure you can answer it, but it's one that's puzzled me for quite some time now.

Mezreth:

The world is a large place. It moves, even the invisible walls shift on the rock and water. For every one known place in this world, there are a thousand hidden places, right?

Steve:

That's interesting and fits because that does make sense to me. I have seen videos of flocks of birds where you can see a group of six birds flying and that's being filmed.

And then in the one frame there's only five birds. And that missing bird didn't go down or up, but it was flying with the others and then it's just vanished. So they go to the hidden places that we no longer see or know of. That hidden place makes unexpected sense to me. Alright then, we've done the birds. We know that they do die, we all do. But where is this hidden place? That's a bonus destination we must start looking for.

Let's talk about another mob that lives around here and I've got a suspicion this group of life form is rare in the cosmos. I've been told this quite a few times. We're now just beginning to understand the complexity, interrelationship and awareness of trees. We're starting to find now that when there's a sick tree, the trees alongside will send more food to it to try and look after it.

And when there's young trees, they feed them more just like we would and out of this new research I'm starting to feel like there's a tribe out there of trees. We're beginning to realize that trees communicate and interact with each other. My question is, can that interaction extend further than just within themselves?

That's where I want to go. And in particular, I want to look at one form of that communication, which is quite radical. And I want to see how we get a reaction to that. We've been told by two psychics that the ancient no forehead skull, which we are custodians of, that it was called a long time ago to this planet.

Now, this is where it gets difficult even for me still to this day. But it wasn't called by hominids and not even by what we mistakenly call Reptilians. It was the trees, this is what I was told twice. That the trees called these aliens to this planet because it was being devastated, it was being destroyed, the trees were being attacked, war and pollution was rife, and the trees collectively called them to help. Is that possible? And if it is, how did the trees communicate with beings on the other side of the cosmos? Because that is a huge leap in everything, even for me.

Mezreth:

One tree is simple. Pulled apart molecule by molecule, the lifeform is almost mechanical. Just like a single neuron. However, only when you bundle them, a connection forms, information is exchanged and assimilated to the point where they begin to change themselves in the universal world around them. That one tree is so much more than it was before. It is part of a web and the stronger the web, the greater their song.

Steve:

So, if you get a large forest, you get more of a reaction and stronger song.

But when you put a group of trees together then you're creating something similar to a brain. One neuron in our brain on its own doesn't amount to much, it needs company.

If all the trees on this planet collectively sent out an S.O.S. in combination, it could travel anywhere. That's how they did it.

Let's go on to the next form of life on this planet. And this is where some people will find this challenging. But of course, I don't when it comes to rocks, I have no issue with that.

But some people might find this difficult. Let's talk about the next form of life, which is when we think about it, the planet. In this solar system we have rock planets and gas planets. You don't have organic life on a gas planet. You can only have that form of life on rock planets. Rocks are the building blocks of life. And I'm wondering if they are life of their own.

And that's what we're going to talk about now. the next question is, before any organic life existed here, there were rocks. Without them, there would have never been any Earthly organic life. The rocks we have are aware and they have both energy and magic. We're aware of that. And a lot of the people we're talking to are also equally aware of that. The question I've got is, that awareness, energy and magic we have experienced, is that force in them which has been there from the beginning or through the actions and ceremonies of humans, or is it somewhere in between?

Mezreth:
Life is not restricted to just biological lifeforms. There is far more life out there than you believe. Life existed here long before organic life grew. Everything is affected by something, and that energy embeds itself into anything close with enough years of energy. A simple pebble can hold enough information to summon a soul and a song.

Steve:
In other words, a piece of rock has the ability to become a receptacle. All the people that touch it, they can make a deposit or withdrawal if the rock is willing and person in congress with the rock is worthy.

So, we have killing rocks that have been used to kill, rocks that can heal humans and rocks that can enlighten, each sacred rock we have has a role to play in the affairs of people.

In concluding this session, I want to leave the rocks for now and return to us. First up, is there any distinguishing feature or ability humans have that separates us from all other earthly lifeforms?

Mezreth:
The belief that humans are singular is the only difference. Arrogant ignorance is what makes you distinguished.

Steve:

That's brilliant. That's not much of a recommendation from Mezreth. There's nothing I can really add to that because it succinctly sums up our greatest flaw.

I can't argue against it either because all the other animals on this planet, I was told this change that is taking place has no impact on any animal except humans. They're all ready for it. We are the only ones who aren't ready and for some this will never be. It's because we do think we're different and superior. And if we started to realize that if we're going back to an Original/ Indigenous/Pagan way, no-one would dare place themselves above any form of life.

What has been lost in translation is that we are all animals, not just sapiens, but all hominids are part of one family. And that truth leads on to the question as to why one strand out of at least sixteen hominids prevailed, all others mysteriously became extinct at around about 12,000 years ago? We know that the Neanderthals, the Denisovans and so many others all disappeared at around that time. Let's be honest, and I've said this often, we were not the smartest of the sixteen 'kids on the block', not by a long shot.

In fact, my latest calculations based on skull sizes ranks us at number six. There are no less than five hominids in front of us. And most probably when they find more, we will slip further down the pecking order. The scientists will tell you these ridiculous stories that we were smarter the Neanderthals and Denisovans, and they know that is clearly untrue.

Their skulls are bigger. This is a very important question. Why is it we survived, and they didn't? Is it simply because our genetic strand was the most pliable and accommodating for alien species to mould and manipulate? Or is it something else?

Mezreth:

The others aren't extinct. They have biologically survived into the soup of humanity. Cast away the illusion of uniqueness. There are many worlds who consider themselves to be the only ones like them. Each one of them, like humanity, are a blend and are surviving. They and you are living dreams of ancient genius. You assume you are a singular thing, but you already were many things long before you became humans. We were all born to different stars. But each of us came from the same place.

Steve:

If Denisovans were extinct, why is it I am 4.7% genetically Denisovan? So, if using my genetic analysis as a baseline they can't be extinct. And nearly everyone on this planet except Africans, have Neanderthal genes in them. Which means they're not extinct. This is scientific evidence validating Mezreth's claim we are them as we merged into one species.

The Original people of this country are known as having a higher percentage of Denisovans than anyone else on the planet. Which means we still carry that genetic legacy.

I think we've covered that topic fairly well. Lea, is there anything else that you think you need to add about what he said during this session?

(Lea adding commentary):

There's a couple things, one of which I wanted to kind of go into little bit more detail in regards to when he was talking about Ezonians., Even though you have all these different species they look different and behave differently, but there is still something that transcends.

There is a bond there. There is a connection that transcends the physical. There is actually a biological relationship between all of us and that's sort of like the description I was telling you about with humanity being a genetic soup of itself, but this applies to others.

I would like to give you an idea of how complex the Ezoni (an E.T. species.) still are. The Ezoni have far more diverse ethnicities among their own than there are with humans. There is really a very, very diverse physical variation present. But they're one group, one people who are the same. But you know, another crazy thing is that

I've been told by Mezreth that there is human DNA in other races, in other species.

Steve:
Yeah. And that contradicts a mistaken assumption that E.T.s who come from one planet all look the same, and that's ingrained in us and it's not the case. They're all different, like us. And our genes have travelled outside this planet. There is not one pure genetic strand that runs through the whole of one planet.

(Lea adding commentary):
The Xannians/Xanik(another E.T. species) are exceptions, but there's actually an unfortunate reason why they are suffering . They're experiencing an evolutionary inverted triangle in reaching a genetic 'dead-end.'. For Xannians, they may well become extinct.

Steve:
So they're running into a genetic cul-de-sac because there's not enough diversity within their genetics.

(Lea adding commentary):
Yes, but that was because of their own horrible doing. And it's a very sad story that you think that humans are the only ones who are capable of genocide. Their descendants who are alive today are suffering because of those extremely unfortunate choices. They're the only exceptions that I know of.

Steve:
I have heard, but cannot verify, the same thing, that the Greys are also genetically becoming stagnant because there's not enough variety within their population. They are breeding themselves into extinction. So, if you don't keep your genetics open to new avenues and genes, there is a tragic and inevitable payback. We've learned one thing from that. We're no different.

The underlying moral of this session is that all animals are our brothers and sisters. There are equals and that runs all the way down the so-called pecking order. We may live longer than most other animals here, but that does not mean we are smarter because of this longevity. Octopi only live for a year. Despite the short life span they're one of the smartest animals in the sea. They live for one year, they're born intelligent. So, we're starting to learn here. The reason is because they are no different, their souls are no different to ours. And that's the moral of the story.

But remember do not stop at the organic, because we've got to include the rocks, and all the other things (and that includes the rings from Atlantis and Lemuria) that make up different forms of intelligence.

Transcript Seven

Steve:

Question number one stems out of an article I read in Duncan Road's magazine, Nexus. It was an interview, I think, with a lady called Linda Mall or something like that. And it was a question-and-answer session with one alien. And it went like this. One area of discussion related to how aliens genetically modified humans.

Now I have no issue with that concept, but in Australia, as opposed to elsewhere, I've always been of the opinion it was a partnership by consent and was steeped in equality. And this is where this gets a bit tricky for me. Basically, the premise was they took a very crude and less intelligent hominid to see whether it could be bred up to be more intelligent and aware. Is it as simple as this or there are nuances not raised?

Mezreth:

That's true, but there have been a few that have altered your development. Our original model, what my kin had intended for you, was different from what you are now. You have also been touched by the Zanashj and those that live outside.

Steve:

So it is basically correct, but the additions are far more diverse and clearly some were not in the original plan.

I have to interject before going further, as the next question is basically a repeat of what was asked in the last transcript, and I forgot that it was asked earlier. Once realising this error my first reaction was to delete this section, but there is a comment made in Mezreth's reply that is new and opens up another field, and more importantly confirms an interpretation Frederic Slater made in reading the engravings at Burragurra. So, bear with the repetition as there is an extension that needs to be absorbed. Scientific papers have tried to come to grips with the issue as to why of the no less than sixteen different types of hominids, Homo sapien sapiens prevailed.

There are suggestions, some incredibly convoluted trying to explain why this happened. Some claim our chins were responsible for our continuation, another suggestion is that our fat cells have given us that extra advantage. So, the big question is why is it all the other hominids aren't here, but we are. What happened to them?

Mezreth:
The other types have never become extinct. They survived in modern humans. Your biological tools allowed you to prevail many changes, and they were given to you by nature and by us. Remember, we blended ingredients, but nature incubated.

Steve:
I have commented on this general proposition already, but said nothing about the last sentence, that is a new extension worthy of further reflection and serious consideration. Frederic Slater stated in his reading of the Buragurra engravings that man was brought to Earth then placed in a "deep sleep from which they were awakened in the prime of life. They found themselves surrounded by glorious game abounding ..." What happened during that time of stasis and how long it lasted is unknown, but there is a considerable gap and that is in complete accord with what Mezreth knows to be true. How this came to pass is still unknown, but what is less debatable is that if you look at the different ancient artifacts, Dreaming stories, paintings and archaeology in Australia, there was earlier times when aliens and humans lived on Earth together and we've made that clear before.

If so, when and why did that cohabitation cease?

Mezreth:
This was a time of Atlantis when that separation really began this issue. Atlantia, we lived together here and now there as the culture

changed. So did the hearts and minds, paranoia and pride eat away at the Atlanteans. They wanted to be stars. Warnings were given but the stars closed their eyes and then they remained closed.

Steve:

Clearly warnings were given. Lea, I do remember you saying when you talked about this on earlier occasions, you did say there were aliens living in Atlantis. And just before the change when Atlantis lost its way and the crystals blew up, they just left without fanfare or fuss in the years before. They didn't really give any explanation as to why they were going. They just quietly absconded. Will there be a time in the foreseeable future when the Aliens will return to this planet and live with us again?

Mezreth:

We want to share this interstellar community with you once again. But we need assurances you will open your eyes. If you cannot then you cannot, then it will only be you who suffers.

Steve:

So, if we open our eyes, it will happen. And if we keep our eyes closed, which is what they are at the moment, there's no reason for them to come. My take on this is if this change is successful and it takes place, the people who are left would be the ones who are deserving to "open their eyes."

Our future is still in our hands.

And for those who don't know and haven't heard this before, there were a group of non-Alien terrestrial beings that left this planet a long, long time ago. And they behaved pretty poorly from what I can gather after they left. But we won't criticize them for that because our track record on this planet is no better.

It would seem this place has hosted many types of beings, some originate from here, while others do not. The other beings born here, what do they actually look like? What did they look like? And how do they regard us?

Mezreth:
Earth has been a home to many beings. Some have been transient and were born there. They have left in crafts and others walked away from the world. You will reunite them again. They wait by the shining dog Sirius.

Steve:
Oh, hence the connection to Sirius. Egyptians were obsessed by Sirius. The ones who live on Sirius, are they the most human-like in appearance? I suppose his reply hints at a yes.

During the long period of time when sapiens lived along so many of the different types of hominids, the portrayal is that we actually wiped them all out because we were better at stabbing people, being devious and violent. That's what we're being told. Was it a peaceful or warlike existence between these different hominids? If there were mainly times of conflict, where were the sapiens positioned in the fighting pecking order?

Mezreth:
Conflict is what drives a soul to change. For better or worse, there was conflict, but there was also peace. However, when these groups fell in love with their greatness, the conflicts turned to wars, and any semblance of peace was the first to become extinct.

Steve:
Now let's talk about the soul Mezreth never leaves alone, and the journey it takes when separating from the body. I know the ancient Egyptians, Original people and Gnostics have a belief that upon death, the soul splits into three. One portion is purely physical, which ceases to exist upon death. But, of the other two parts, half goes into a place of rest, reflection, and perhaps reincarnates. And we come back yet again, if we choose to.

That destination of refection and accountability most people will accept, some people call it Heaven, Bliss or Nirvana, it doesn't really matter about names or titles. Now this is where it gets complicated, as the other half goes back in the country, a sacred site or even bones, and if not, it returns into what Yung refers to as the collective unconscious. Is that belief true or false?

Mezreth

The soul departs to a place for reflection. The body returns to the land so that the soul may have a chance to live again. Today you are breaking that cycle.

Steve:

"Today you are breaking that cycle." Isn't that about what's supposed to take place in this Earthly ascension in that many people can't come back? Isn't that what he's actually indirectly saying? Because isn't that what that change is supposed to be about? Are we supposed to be trying to make a connection with the land? That's what the Hopi prophets said. To become part of the Old Teachings is the prime priority and future direction. And we've only got a certain amount of time left to do this.

What he's saying right now, is that we have a chance, not that it is freely given, it has to be earnt. And if you don't fix it up, you can't incarnate back there. That turns out to be an actual affirmation of the whole underlying belief of what we think is happening.

In making the right choice it seems to me we are inherently handicapped, as our experts assure us that we use up the 15% of the brain and the rest does nothing beyond spectating, and they also claim the same ratio applies to our genes. And it has always been like this. Basically, if I was to compare that illogical diagnosis to a car, you got one and a quarter cylinder working and six and three quarters marking time. Has that always been the case or is this just something that has occurred in recent times?

Mezreth:

Yes, but you can learn how to use more parts. You have the potential for psionics. However, with the right training and manifesting, many more doors will fly open so and actually there is a further answer.

(Lea adding context):
It seems like we are fixed to a certain amount of usage. However, what we could do before was use more, we could section parts off of our brain to actually use more parts effectively. When he's talking about science, we still have that. We still have the predisposition, we can still do it.

It's just that no one's ever been able to teach us. No-one has really been able to give us an elementary this is how you do that. In order to effectively use your brain because we are not shown how to use our brains, we're not actually taught how to unlock the areas of our brain that have fallen into deer coma. What we are taught is how to memorise answers and keep up with our neighbours and those people who fit in.

Who is going to tell me what to do to make sure that I take the right supplements or do the right brain exercises? In the schools and universities, we are never really taught how to use every part of the fraction remaining effectively.

But it is worth remembering that if you use a whole thing 100% and you switched all of that on, we would either have a fit or it would kill us instantly..

Even electrical machines can fizzle out if they have too much electricity pumping through them. And that'll happen to us.

Steve:
And what that means is the Department of Education's in different states and countries around the world are protecting humans by making sure they use a small fraction of their brain, and therefore, we won't overload and implode. Some may feel they are dumbing us down completely and are driven by the wrong intentions, but no, they're saving us from the possibility of thinking too much.

So really, we should thank the Department of Education because I thought the content and obsession with exams was just mindless repetition with no chance to ask a question or think outside the box but is something far more benevolent. Because this safety-first preventative approach will ensure that we will never have a meltdown (or intelligent independent thought).

(Lea adding commentary):
Yeah, it's stupidity. It's not, it's not necessarily deliberately keeping somebody stupid. There's is more to this, it's about those who in control using every power to its maximum potential to damage and stifle without suffering the consequences of this hideous assault on innocent children. Children at school deserve to be nurtured and expanded, but it slowly turns into is all about rote-taught compliance and subservience.

We are our brain, and it is the control panel for our spirits. Our soul is that the pilot, but if the brain is weak and obedient it sacrifices its independence to those who control, and the pilot will have trouble navigating or even moving.

Steve:
That does indirectly lead into the last question. Karno W. often said that there was a time back when we used a lot more of our DNA than we do now. But that's not actually quite right, and it is not quite what he meant.

What he meant was that we had a lot of DNA that we did use effectively, and we can't anymore. It is suffering the same fate as our brain, both are running on empty and damaged because of this. He said that all the sacred rocks with clear evidence of advanced technology were made during these ancient times when our genes and brain were thriving. We had a greater understanding of the capacity of our brain and a greater idea of how to excel.

(Lea adding commentary):
If you're constantly told that you can't do this, how are you expected to ever be able to do it. So, it's like if you're not taught something you can't be expected to know.

Steve:

The best way to do something, especially with the children, because as we know they still have parts of those areas of their brain that are more mystical and magical ready and willing if engaged, is encourage children to seek out visions and stay in contact with their 'imaginary friends.' As a counter the experts and adults have to convince the child sees and hears from across the divide is not there. It didn't happen, it's a make-believe friend. We've all heard that one. And so many children get told they're looking at and hearing their imagination or themselves. And what we to do is make sure that we totally repress the psychic talents at the start of a child's life and it is only when that is done and dusted they're ready to live in the adult 'real world.'.

Strangely enough this etheric theme was originally a central part of language and that is especially so when dealing with the first language spoken. We often make mention of the Original First Language that was spoken around the world in ancient times. And if people don't believe that there was one global language in ancient times, we suggest you go to the Bible. There is extensive talk about the Tower of Babylon. When there was a time when everyone could speak one language, then they didn't.

Is that a metaphor, or is it a literal statement of a truth?

Well, my question is, was there a First Language spoken around the planet?

Mezreth:

The first language is thought, understanding oneself and one's surroundings to communicate these concepts beyond telepathy is beholden to thought like mathematics is beholden to logic, the desire to understand one surroundings. The first language is the tongue of the soul.

Steve:

That could be telepathy. Or it could be another way non-five-sensory method of communicating. Frederic Slater is adamant that the Original First Language was called "Soul Language" and that it was given to humans by the Sky-Heroes. What cannot be questioned is that the Bible has a very detailed and graphic record of how there was a common global tongue and once this was discontinued strife, discord, and warfare became the new norms. The problem was that once people from different areas spoke in different languages, they could no longer understand each other and required another to interpret and represent.

Transcript Eight

Steve:

I want to start this session with three quotes from Edgar Cacey and hopefully responses from you as to whether he was right or wrong and why. First up, Cacey did originally think that astrology was bogus and of no substance. And to be honest, up until quite recently, I was inclined to think the same way or give it very little serious consideration. That's changed. Casey was shocked by two things that were in his readings while sleeping, the word reincarnation, and the other offending utterance was astrology, because he was a devout Christian, those things just don't belong.

And he had a lot of issues dealing with his content. But this is what he actually said. This is what the sleeping prophet kept returning to. During these sessions that spanned across so many curtains he told those in attendance that the stars represent soul patterns. The twelve signs of the Zodiac are twelve patterns, from which the soul chooses when coming onto the earth. They relate to races, patterns of temperament, personality, etc. Is he correct?

Mezreth:

Don't worry. He is not right in his conclusions. But you must remember the outer universe is a reflection of the inner universe. And if the heart bends, the hand follows. The universe moves in spite for you, in love for you, and always around you.

Steve:

In other words, Cayce was not right in his conclusion. It doesn't mean the parameters are wrong. So, what he's saying was a bit about the heart that was quite stunning. So does that mean you are put into these patterns, but they're not set in stone, and you can change them. It's a symbiotic relationship. It goes both ways.

We can change those patterns, temperaments and personality if we want. So that is a force, but it's not a force that can make us do something. It's just a force we can react to and maybe react against if we don't want it anymore.

I really like that one. The heart bends and hand follows. That's really quite clever and adds a little bit of perspective to the next part of Cayce's prophecy. Mezreth is not denying the fact that there is an influence. He's denying that we are actually prisoners to that, so that links in with something else.

Cayce claimed that in every 2160 years, a different age of the Zodiac is in position that dominates the earth. It goes backward and therefore is called a procession. During the heyday of Egypt, the sign of Taurus the bull was the commanding position. So the people of Egypt worshipped the bull.

And that's really got me, as it were, it was an overt sign. The sun was actually in Scorpio and was shining across Taurus. He's saying that influence is global, maybe even cosmic, as opposed to just personal.

Mezreth:
The only universe that we have any semblance of control over is the one on the inside. And if you can master that, then the rest follows.

Steve:
It's the same across the board. He doesn't recognize a difference. So, when you're talking about a collective through to the individual, the lines he describes are very, very blurred, because they're all the same. Whether it's the internal universe or the world, it's the same thing.

And you already explained how this works, how to first work on the microcosmic level which then puts you in a position where you can change if you wish. Then the same thing must apply at a different level.

.

.

This reminds me of a scene in a show called Friends where the girl with the blond hair, Phoebe, is talking to Joey. She was patting Joey on the head, consoling him because he said he couldn't remember anything about his past lives. And she said, "well, that's no surprise" because "you're a brand-new soul." At the time I thought that line was mildly amusing at the time.

I did give some credence to this comment. We often hear this comment passed on to someone who is not aware or insightful, as being a young soul.

However, Cacey says that all of the souls God created came into existence at the very beginning, and none have been made since. It seems everything is timeless, was Casey right or wrong to say that all souls were made at the beginning?

Mezreth:
Our souls are broken and forged, absorbed and separated at all times. There is no beginning. And there is no end. The only time is a circle of eternity. A piece of stone, as it is, may be a mere eon, but the energy of the stone is timeless. Just as my soul may be an eon, the age of my energy is forever.

Steve:
That's actually a stunning answer, if "the energy of a stone is timeless," that must also apply to the souls of everything. It seems that this time Cayce was correct.

With the soul created at the beginning, I wanted to return to the nature and duality of the soul, in particular what the ancient Egyptians, Gnostics, and Original Dreaming and now Cayce reluctantly also stated. Now, he didn't say it specifically because he's a Christian, but in the end of one sleeping session he talked about the soul. He spoke about being broken into two separate parts.

But it's very specific. He was saying what I said. That one half of the soul moved beyond the curtain to reflect and consider will most likely be reincarnated in the future, while the other half stayed behind going into the country or what Jung would call the collective unconscious. Bearing in mind Mezreth did say that souls are broken, reforged, split up and moved around.

Within all that movement and separation, it reunites with the other half when it returns to take on a new life on this planet. Is this correct?

Mezreth:
Upon death, an explosion of consciousness happens. It pours into everything. And everyone who is around the deceased, partially embeds itself into the relative material world around it, but the surviving soul, it departs if chooses to do so. Some choose to linger and bond with their old world. Some are lost and others wander.

Steve:
I'm not sure whether Mezreth is agreeing with an actual division as such, but I'm going to take that as close to yes.

Irrespective of how the soul is constituted when we incarnate in on this planet, we lose most to nearly all of our awareness and knowledge of heaven or nirvana while in bodily form.

I've been told by Lea, that Mezreth has incarnated in bodily form.

When he did this, when he came to this planet, did the same rules apply? Did he lose the big picture knowledge, which is what that is? Or did he retain all of it, or somewhere in between?

And if he did, how is this possible? Because I thought that there is a rule that when you came here, you had to be tested by being prompted into a leap of faith. So, the question is, what state of awareness did he bring across with him?

Mezreth:
It doesn't matter what new life a soul reincarnates into. They will never be able to remember every memory of their past lives. However, one must be open to the memories peeking through, not shying away. No matter how heartbreaking the memory, the more you pull away, the less your current mind will be able to remember.

There are many reasons why someone cannot recall their past lives. They refuse to do so. They don't understand what they are.

And for others, they have a thick haze wrapped around their souls that stops them. My old life, I viewed the world through a keyhole. I was ignorant by accident and arrogant by choice. I made many mistakes for my soul to learn from. But those mistakes are being paid by others. That's why I'm here. My perspective was narrow then, so it may be wider now.

Steve:

Oh really? So, to an extent he did go into this mortal life carrying very little with him. He did lose something and that's the deal. And he took those experiences as things to make him a better person. If he hadn't had those lives, he would not be wiser now. He was using this place not only just to guard and take an interest in, but also to use like we all do as a school, a place to learn lessons. That would mean it would be absolutely a blessing not to remember.

(Lea adding commentary):

I do not necessarily agree. I think no. To understand where you are, you have to know what happened before if you want to know where you're going now, you have to know how to get there. The thing is, I remember my past lives because my measures taught me how to remember the past lives. So, we all have that memory. But in some respects, if we broke into it, it would probably overwhelm us.

I want to make one observation as an aside. What I find fascinating was is that in Edgar Cayce's case, in his last life he was a general who was involved in killing people. He was responsible for the deaths of many people and had no compunction to continue killing throughout his life. It's interesting how some people might have this idea that people who had great intentions and deeds, who some regard as saints, have always been saints, but that isn't always so. While everyone knows Casey was a stunning human being, but few know in a past life he was fully involved in warfare and killing.

Just like Mezreth said, he may have came out of that dreadful experience by learning some of the final lessons he had to learn and came back the next time a better person.

Steve:

Basically, while incarnated here, you don't know anything about the other side. Therefore, everything you do is either a leap of faith or a leap of the wrong way.

Mezreth for reasons I am sure he will or may reveal in the future, has shared details of some of my past-lives. But not only the outlines but specifics and inner motivations were spoken of. I actually thought, and told this to Lea often, that knowing so much of her past was an incredible burden to bear, never expecting I was soon to go through the same process. What did throw me was that he knew of my actions and intentions, which I'm not going to talk about because that's not really on point. All of this leads up to a question that has been ever-present how is it possible to create such an intimate contact while he is existing somewhere completely differently from where I am at that particular moment in time? How can you do that? How can you actually read other people like that and know what they've done?

Mezreth:

Souls move together in each life, like a herd. We know each other now because we knew each other before. Each of us were friends, lovers and enemies. The phenomena of eternity.

Steve:

The Original Dreaming believes that the spirits are everywhere, and can see everything you do and know why, which is exactly what he said in a completely different way. Now, it's not a completely different way. It's the same way. And he said souls move together in a herd. I've seen herds and flocks flawlessly veer, swerve and vary speed simultaneously, they are obviously sharing their thoughts, so nothing is hidden. What logically follows is that if you did something wrong and you kept it a secret, then the spirits would make sure the secret would soon be public knowledge. There'd be a sign in the clouds, or a bird would tell someone else, and you would become unstuck because of it.

There are no secrets, even the ones we keep will find an audience.

While addressing the issue of secrets, I'd like to once again make this personal in trying to analyse a form or manner of existence to Mezreth, is your existence in a spiritual or mortal form? Lea has told me you're both, which in itself is difficult to comprehend, but there is some form of flesh and bone in your equation.

So, if he inhabits a mortal body I would assume his body, like ours, dies. And if doesn't, why not? And secondly, what is his major form of existence?

Mezreth:
From the beginning, my kin can do both. Some choose permanence of one. We all age, but only a few of us have chosen to die. Be grateful for your brief lives, for you can transcend faster and experience divinity sooner.

Steve:
If they don't choose to die, then their body can't decay. By inference, that has to happen. And if they choose to die and only a few have chosen to die, does that mean that a lot of people mistake them as being angels. I read sections of an old book called the Bible a few times. And in it, angels are supposed to fly, and they're supposed to be tall and ageless. And beyond being eternal, which many humans would crave for, he then said we were luckier because we didn't go through this ageless process. Put all of this together and I start to see how this notion of holy angels came about.

(Lea adding context):
It is because of their timeless life expectancy these angels envy us. They might be known by other names. Because their life expectancy

is so long that to us it may seem essentially immortal, but they're not immortal simply due to the fact they can choose to die.

However, he has said to me several times that they have lived for so long that they don't actually know what their real-life expectancy is. And because they've been around for so long, some individuals of his race have deliberately chosen to end their lives sooner.

Steve:
That's amazing. So, they don't know what their life expectancy is because most have never reached it, for them death never happened unless they forced the issue. Would that explain why there are a lot of myths eulogising what many claim to be the fountain of youth. This quest that enables humans to live forever, coupled with medical experts claiming that aging is a disease, not a process itself, opens up all sorts of possibilities.

Either way, whether dying or never dying while deposited on this same mortal plane, there are three things that came to mind. Does he eat, does he sleep, and can he experience pain?

Mezreth:
Of course. Well, without pain, we cannot know joy or boundaries. We eat and sleep if we choose to do so.

(Lea adding context):
Yeah, they are alive, but they're barely physical. I mean, they do have physical presence, but their needs are so far removed from anything that we have. It's essentially like it's true alien. If you asked me, my take is that they absorb energy. But they don't need to eat in the conventional ways we understand and digest.

They don't have to eat and don't have to drink. They don't need to sleep. They don't have to, but they do rest when they're absorbing energy. Above these more basic needs, they do experience a tremendous amount of pleasure and pain.

For us, we divide our experiences and sensations into the mental and physical. To them, it's same thing. They don't have nerves like we have, but they do experience a tremendous amount of pain. And he says without it, we cannot know joy or establish boundaries.

Steve:
I'm still stuck on the phrase "if we chose to." For us it is not a choice but compulsory, for his kind it is the ultimate extension of the oft heard mantra of freedom of choice. Now we have dispensed with the physical side of Mezreth's existence, and am none the wiser, I would like to talk about what Mezreth's main focus and possible reason he chose not to die as some of his kind preferred. Are there some earthly incarnated souls that you take more interest in? Because there's quite a few on the planet right now. There's around seven billion plus of them. And I can't imagine that he's taking personal interest in all seven billion, because that would do your head in.

What is it about the souls you chose to work with that makes it worth the effort?

Mezreth:
There have been many because they remind us of ourselves, of where we were, where we are now, and where we want to be, all things.

Steve:
Where we want to be, that is really something I did not expect in the least. From my perspective we are so far behind and below, but not so, and here is a statement I never expected, there is something about us they admire and strive to reach. That was a surprise because I thought they were light-years in front of us on every conceivable level.

Then again this has been such an incredibly difficult testing ground compared to the other incarnations on other planets, because it is so difficult here, Mezreth has said this also, maybe this place really does bring the best and worst out of eveybody.

Trying to identify what they want to reach and copy, now that is a task and a half. But amongst the chaos and dross there are hints and shining lights out there.

I do know and personally saw Karno actually disappearing, and I know for a fact he did vanish.

It is a great way to conclude on such a positive note, that we, as a collective have some admirable qualities, and knowing that after the ceremony at Uluru the planet is about to transform, we need all the positive energy we can muster. I know I've asked this before, but I haven't asked it in this way or context. We've got a few months to go. What advice would you give all human beings during these turbulent times right now? What advice would you give knowing that my understanding is that things are running to a conclusion. Has he got any advice or gems of wisdom he can pass on so we can pass this on to others? .

Mezreth:
Don't lie to yourselves.

Transcript Nine

Steve:

Lea, I remember before you mentioned Elzona is a planet that has incredible music and art on it – according to you it is better than here. My question to Mezreth is why is there such a unique artistic dynamic on earth? In music, you have rock, jazz, country, rap, etc. and so many different people like so many different genres. The same diversity and taste exist in art also. Is this kind of diversity unique on earth?

Mezreth:

Elzona is a world even my kin question why we decided to add our children on its face. That world's secrets lay deeper than her core. It is a very strange world, there are far more mysteries there than on earth. Ezoni (the guardians of Elzona, much like humans are guardians of earth) have unmatched diversity in their art and much of their inspiration comes of the dynamic, wonderful and terrifying mysteries of their beloved world: Elzona. Why do they create so much? Because they can create, whereas humans gave themselves permission to destroy.

(Lea adding context):

Mezreth and his group actually created life on that planet, too, much like over here. They have had a lot of influence and made their own alterations as well to the Ezoni (predominant species there) of the planet.

Steve:

Well, that is a bit disappointing as I had us in first place throughout the Universe. My thinking was the art and music was what Mezreth's mob were so attracted to, turns out we are second best or even worse. It seems to me if we want to catch up and narrow the gap, we have dumped our addiction to destroying. From my biased point of view, I'd like to add to that lightening of the musical garbage in banning disco, rap and quite a lot of country and western music

This really is one massive cosmic laboratory, an experiment with a rock and water petri dish, but it's cosmic, not earthly. That's the interesting part of this.

On this planet we've got millions of organisms, seven billion different faces, so many types of geology, geography, and vegetation, everything is so massively varied.

There's so much that's going on. And my question is, is this countless diversity the cosmic norm or exception?

Mezreth:

The only extremes on Earth are the psychological, you live in a cooking pot of dangerous and beautiful. These extremes breed extremes. However, don't mistake this as a negative it is essential for you to find the balance within yourselves and understand the why. Only then you can understand us.

Steve:

. What Mezreth is agreeing to is that this is a melting pot of extremes, not just on a genetic and physical level, but this is merely a reflection of what lays beneath and what's inside. Of recent there is one extremity that has really ramped up, which is fear and violence.

And if you think about it, the ways that we've killed other people, the different techniques and weapons used is almost unbelievable. It used to be a long time back a spear, knife or blade was the sum total on hand.

I read an article in Nexus featuring an interview with an alien who made the claim that trees are very rare in the in this universe.

Equally, there are reports and rumours maintaining that the trees on this planet were once miles high. Is this true?

Mezreth:

Trees, like biological life, are technically a cosmic rarity. Only technically because there's no biological life on Mars and Uranus,

Jupiter, Pluto, Mercury. It's a majority that don't have biological life. However, worlds with biological life, trees are not a cosmic rarity in in that scope. It's true that trees on Earth are biologically unique, like on a Elzona, like on Xann and many more.

The trees on Earth were meant to evolve to a greater consciousness biosphere. However, they are sadly, putting in efforts to adapt to modern human meddling to the naked human eye. Trees appear to be mere mechanical organisms, simple and unassuming. However, they can communicate across a whole continent to many different organisms faster, and more effectively than the phone. The biological internet.

Steve:

That's really quite fascinating and the part that resonated the most is that trees on this planet were meant to evolve to a higher level of consciousness than trees elsewhere in the cosmos.

Right now, collectively humans sit near the bottom rung. As we said often, both Elders and psychics have told us that the no-forehead beings we are researching were called to the Earth because of a distress call put out by the trees, and if Mezereth is correct in calling trees a "biological internet" that is entirely feasible.

And if the trees were meant to evolve to a greater consciousness than anywhere else, is that what this planet is about, also? And the fact that he knew the answer from the time you basically gave a couple of words, says a lot about the importance of trees.

(Lea adding context):

And if I may add a little bit, because it's something that he has discussed many times with me as well with other of my contacts, but with him particularly, because I have the most communication with him. He talks of not just humans. But all of the other intelligent lifeforms on other worlds and he doesn't think of us as residents or even the true natives of Earth.

He looks at us as guardians, as doormen/women, of the building acting as a security guard. You don't live there. You are meant to protect it. You just happen to be born there. You work there, you happen to live your lives here. But you are not the owners. You do not own this place. You are supposed to be serving and tending for this place.

Steve:

Yeah, that makes sense to me. And that's what we're here to do. And of course, the trees are part of this place. And we don't see this truth anymore, but the Indigenous people did. And now we've found out the trees were meant to evolve to a greater consciousness than anywhere else, so as guardians we are doing a dreadful job. And we've got to start realizing that and if we don't improve our performance and intentions, we will have to vacate the premises.

Let's leave the distress of the trees and return to the cause of their grief, humans. Dolores Canon said that the timing of incarnation into a foetus baby is not that specific. She said that the soul might occupy the newly growing body from the point of conception up until the time it is taking its first breath, which means this could happen once the baby leaves the mother.

Mezreth:

It can depend on how quick the soul decides to occupy the foetus. The most common time for soul entering a growing pineal gland in a human host averages for two months. But there are many different organisms with different gestation periods. But this is specifically talking about humans and also depends on how steadfast that soul is to actually occupy.

Some tend to want to linger around until the right time comes around the potential parent and potential body, and then it links in with it.

Steve:

What I found interesting is that at two months, nearly all the organs in your body are in embryonic form or not even formed at that stage. And it is here and then that we are enter the body via the pineal gland, which we know is supposed to be the spiritual centre of our body.

And that's their entry point. Not the stomach, not the liver, not the heart, but the pineal gland. That is interesting. I think in some cases with stillborn children, that could be a case where the soul has made the decision not to return.

Cayce was a devout Christian and had a real issue, with the content he supplied while asleep. Who was in contact with Cayce? Was it God, an angel, a spirit or one of your mob?

Mezreth:
My kin and I speak to anyone who needs to listen.

Steve:
I think that could mean yes, they were in contact with him. When Edgar Cayce was alive, he didn't know what Atlantis was. That knowledge first came to him when in his meditative and prophetic trances

From that complete state of ignorance in all things Atlantean he then went on to insist that over half the Americans alive had a past life in Atlantis. Is this why there is such a deep fascination with Atlantis? The drawback is that is it advisable to spend so much time trying to rekindle the Atlantean flame, when it is so tainted, while the little known about Lemuria is entirely positive and certainly worth emulating? Could you share with us some of the traits and positives coming out of Lemuria that seem to be lost in translation?

Mezreth:
All modern humans have ties to the golden age of Atlantia. Although not all were Atlanteans. And if Atlantia was the clock and Alkhem was the jewel, then Lemuria was the wand.

Steve:
And there's more to come in this ancient tale so we won't pre-empt what comes next, but I do want to raise the vexed issue of magic,

which I think was pursued to the highest level in Lemuria. I believe this is where the great magicians mastered their esoteric skills. And this is where I believe the tradition of magic was developed and has never left the planet since, even in more recent times in Europe it was what Nostradamus and Merlin practiced in the royal courts.

I believe it's one of the sapien talents things that made us appealing to the Aliens from elsewhere because we did have that skill. Mind you, I've got to make a point about this, and I think it's very important. And that is how it still should be, as we live on one of the most magic rocks in the cosmos. You've got the trees of this place bearing the thwarted potential to be incredibly spiritual. If nothing else, despite the denials and objections each of us will get a taste of magic through absorption if you live on this planet long enough. Some of that magic must seep through. But there are a lot of people trying to stop that.

We know through the dealings we've had with the rings, that I trust implicitly any ring or object that comes from Lemuria. However, any object or ring that comes from Atlantis also has magic, but it is wilful and without a moral compass. Despite all the grief and fall from grace in Atlantis, it has to be remembered that Atlantis began with the most noble and altruistic of intentions.

And that's very important to understand. And its interesting how Cayce was so sure so many Atlanteans are incarnate in America ironically borders, the Atlantic Ocean.

(Lea adding commentary):
We all carry from our own experience's past life memories. We all tend to carry a little bit of that into our present life baggage. Every new life should begin with a clean slate. But depending on the level of trauma, then you're likely to get a little bit of those old feelings, those old mentalities, those old ways of thinking resurfacing in the new life. Which theoretically shouldn't happen, because it's about starting a new setting, a fresh start.

And, you know it's not a shock to me whatsoever, but that so many people, particularly those who live in the US have this unnatural obsession and love towards the Atlantean legend. So much so they named one of their Space Shuttles after this so-called mythical island.

Steve:

The funny part of the mystery is this. If you look at what we know about Atlantis, and it primarily comes through Pliny the Elder and Plato. To that esteemed duo we should also include the Greek poet and writer, Homer. He wrote a poem about Aphrodite, dedicating to her the Atlantean metal Orichalcum. It is the sacred metal used extensively in the Temple of Poseidon and Clieto.

What is common knowledge is that all ancient accounts verify is that Altantis destroyed itself.

(Lea adding commentary):
I was there.

Steve:

You have that bonus, and I might have had something to do with it, but I don't want to cover that here. What is relevant is that everyone's still looking for possible archaeological Atlantean remains and are still talking about this island that literally killed itself on its own sword. It destroyed itself. And there is a quote I've used quite a few times, the basically warns people when seeking out the legacy of Atlantis to look, but don't stare.

I think observation summed it up perfectly. Especially since the spirit and flaws of Atlantis is back and pulsating throughout the planet. The only real difference is the power source we use now is more polluting and filthier than the huge crystals the Atlanteans used. Aprat from that for all intents and purposes apart from the smoke and mirrors it is the same old, same old ...

(Lea adding commentary):
Yes. So, it's still detrimental but in a different way.

Steve:

Perhaps one of the defining issues that leads on to chaos and a disconnection with Mother Nature is the vexed issue of over-population. What was the maximum population of Atlantis and Lemuria?

Mezreth:

Atlantia had tens of millions spanning across the island. Lemuria reached over a million. Lemuria was a place to visit, not to live.

Steve:

That to me is probably one of the most important comments he's made about these two ancient civilisations. It was a place to visit not to live. Now, this really does sound to me to be extremely relevant as we've had these myths forever of an idyllic Shangri-La, Garden of Eden or some type of paradise on Earth. We've always had these legends of this perfect place, it's been in our collective psyche forever.

I want to make that point clear, because at some point it sounds like I'm just running one place down and sanctifying the other. But what I find really interesting, is that Lemuria was a place to visit. Now, I do remember earlier on one occasion we spoke about Australia and Atlantis Mezreth did say more than once that at one stage Atlanteans tried to come to Australia, and they were here for a while then and at some time after were banished and never returned to Lemuria. Which of course is proven by the fact that two of the three Atlantean rings were buried in Australia.

Now that confirms what Mezreth was saying about Lemuria being a place to visit. You can't stay here. Also confirms what I've always known through our archaeology, that the Original people were fully aware of all the technology elsewhere. There's a line in the sand somewhere between both ancient empires, and I think that's the same line in the sand when they were asked to leave and never return to Lemuria.

Let's leave the past and move on to something that is still present in ancient scriptures and modern-day thinking. I wanted to talk about these angels in more detail because there is not a culture, be it indigenous or sedentary, that doesn't acknowledge some sort of supernatural being that is an interlocutor between the creator and us.

Now, some people give the more advanced angelic beings names like the Archangel Michael along with other titles. In all narratives of angels, they are supposed to live forever.

In every account most of them are able to travel long distances quickly, are tall and have humanlike features. Yeah, you can throw wings on some of them, but that might be put there because if I could fly through the air or levitate, depicting wings is symbolically equivalent to having wings.

That description also fits when itemizing the features of yourself, and. your companions. Is that merely a coincidence or is it because you and your kind are the same as angels?

Mezreth:
We copied some of our form over to our children. You adopted your own features over time and impressed what you desire into art, as did we. Vanity is not exclusive to humans. You call many beings angels. I have been referred to as an angel, also a fallen one, neither wrong nor right.

Steve:
Well, it's interesting. He said he's been called an angel from both sides of the fence. Of course, that does not discount the possibility that angels are a separate entity of more etheric ancestry, and that Mezreth and others of his ilk have been mistakenly assumed to be angels. Saying that they are "neither right or wrong" leaves both options open.

(Lea adding commentary):
And it's funny, if we're talking about taking forms, there are all sorts of beings out there that can shapeshift. Essentially, his mob is just one of many that can shapeshift, and they do tend to take on forms that are not human adults, so they could be either children or animals.

Steve:
It's well known. Original people both in America and Australia will tell you that the aliens, when they were here and when they have come here, love the children, and they tend to keep away from the adults. That hints at the possibility that human adults are more dangerous. But of one thing I do know, they love children.

The immediate question that arises out of this preference is that if you're an adult and they don't trust you, but they would they trust you as a child. What happened between being an innocent child and a jaded adult? Something fell apart as we grew and aged. I believe the explanation lies within the education system we have at the moment, which is possibly the most pernicious and evil institution we have on the planet.

From the age of six in Australian schools the tests begin, and do not stop until one final exam. Every year they will be tested and compared against the group. And what are you tested in? Not inquisitiveness, not in curiosity, it's all about what you can memorize and repeat.

If you do those two things, you succeed. Every IQ test is based around one skill, comprehension. If you happen to be a bad reader, you will automatically get a low IQ score.

So therefore, they really are honing in one type of intelligence and saying that overrides everything else. And if your reading skills are not up to scratch, if you're dyslexic or dull and that means according to every approve measurement that you are intellectually slow or maybe even stupid. And that's the way education is today. Essentially what we have now is a competition of everybody against everybody. Where the winner takes all and the losers get nothing.

And the children are now getting accustomed to surviving in a dog-eat-dog society, and by the way, dogs don't eat dogs.

They take away the curiosity and take away the wonder and add a dash of fear, then sprinkle it with competition. What comes out of this is one imperative, you must do better than everyone else in the class. Don't share anything with them and if you play by the school's rules and results, you will eventually turn into an adult with money and prestige. And then the child behaves like an adult, which means behave, stop asking questions and do what you're supposed to do. That's what our education system is. The angels and aliens are aware of that.

My last question in this session is based around something Mezreth said earlier which really resonated with me.

Is there a passage in any scripture that recommends self-loathing as the path to salvation. To an extent I understand why you said this. But we live in a global society where so many lifestyle coaches implore that we have to love ourselves unconditionally, and because of this, many might find your dictum to hate yourself somewhat puzzling.

Could you explain in more detail why you said this?

Mezreth:
Because this is an essential part to spiritual development because you have to identify the wrongs before you can identify the rights. Unfortunately, on Earth, we do have this predilection for self-loathing and so people tend to listen more to self-criticism over self-love first. Self-love is a vehicle to salvation, but not many understand what self-love truly means. So I speak in ways that express clearer parts of this idea for you: you self-hate when you succumb to lounging an hour longer than you want, you self-hate when you continue a forced smile, you self-hate when you tell yourself you are higher and most righteous than all others I express. You must resist these small beliefs. Self-love is doing anything you can to live, not survive, even if it takes you to places of pain.

Steve:

The first step towards self-love is to actually understand what it is you hate. And then don't do it. You've got to acknowledge the fact that there are things you do that you hate, and a lot of people don't.

I've had people tell me on occasions when they've done really bad things, they concoct an escape clause by adding the devil made me do it. And they have actually said that to me more than once. And as I am hearing this I'm thinking, no, no, no, no, it just doesn't work like that. It is your door, and you opened it because you were full of self-loathing and refused to acknowledge "the devil inside." And then, once you opened the door, you said come on in and make yourself a home.

So really, what he's saying is you are your enemy. It's your ego that gets in the way of most of the things that you should be doing. Granted you need to have a little bit of ego to do certain things, like standing on a stage and being confident, but never let your ego become the star attraction.

Transcript Ten

Steve:

Has Australia always been part of Lemuria? Some Original Elders I've spoken to refer to this country as Mu and I've heard others say the same thing. If it is, could you supply a general geographical sketch map of the entire Lemurian continent?

Mezreth:

The freehold of Lemuria stretched from the North Pacific Islands all the way to the shores of Africa. Lemuria was not a city nor a nation. It was a world of its own. Atlantis found their way to the crocodile's nose for many millennia, until they were judged and ultimately expelled.

Steve:

It sounds to me from what I'm hearing that it's not so much a continent per se, but it could be an alliance of islands and the edges of other areas as well. Whatever the lay of the land, it would seem logical to include Australia. That spread of geography does sound similar to the way Atlantis evolved.

(Lea adding context):

Yeah, it would probably be the same. The only difference is with Atlantis even the offshore islands were still considered to be part of Atlantis. Lemuria was different it because not a formal nation. It wasn't a country as such, but more a loose confederation.

Steve:

Obviously, Lemuria includes Original people of Australia, which is one group, and then there are also some Asian and Pacific Island people within this confederation. And even though they do have different cultures, somehow all coexisted.

The next question flows off this to an extent and we're probably going to get roughly the same answer. You said previously that it was sparsely populated compared to Atlantis. What was the main settlement pattern? Was it hunter gatherer, small villages or cities with a capped population?

Mezreth:
Modest tribes were scattered. They had nexus meeting points to discuss and exchange. These points were great places for refuge, but none did make them home. It was home to Lemuria and her invisible children, each nexus point was equally spread for each community. There is a reason why the wise seek solace and the obtuse seek equal company. There is a reason why each member of the pack has a face, and the herd is faceless. Lemuria knew this because Lemuria had told them.

Steve:
Original people mainly lived in clans numbering at around fifty, they would meet with all the other clans that made up one tribal network on common ground for ceremonies, problem solving or when there was a huge supply of food. When they did have tribal meetings, they selected a location agreeable to all clans within the tribe. And even when they have wars, they would never fight on their lands, it would be held on neutral land. So, this sounds to me to be very similar to what took place in Lemuria. And that makes sense as Australia is the largest residual landmass that was originally part of Lemuria.

The reason why I wanted to find out about how each civilisation dealt with increasing population is because the Greeks were insistent that once a city got to population of over 50,000 people, it was doomed to fail and implode on itself.

So, these small villages when they come together at certain times still kept the numbers low, whereas Atlantis clearly did not see large numbers of people gathering together as a problem.

Remaining in Atlantis and Lemuria, Lea you have told us that Atlanteans were fastidious about keeping records and information, this is one of the things that they are renowned for and being that precise with any information, near enough is never good enough.

This omission becomes a big issue. We know that to begin with Atlantis and Lemuria had some form of cooperative arrangement, and he's already said that in an early answer. Then Atlantis no longer had any further contact. But there's no official reason given for severing relations except that no one was allowed to go to Lemuria, but no reason was ever given, and that's just not the way they do things.

This is a monumental separation of the two great world powers, and it really should be recorded in considerable detail. What actually happened?

Mezreth:
Lemuria greets visitors through her law of judgment. It can take a day or a thousand lifetimes, but all are ultimately judged. Make no mistake, Lemurians do not make this choice. They are mere speakers of the land. Lemuria understood something beyond what her guests could see. She read the book and cast her choice in favour for the events to come or against. Never forget Lemuria, she still judges.

Steve:
Mezreth did make it clear earlier that this was not a place where you could move in and say, I want to stay. That is not going to happen.

When expanding upon passing judgment, he's saying it's the land that makes the judgment, not them, they are interlocutors acting as speakers for the land. The Original people would say virtually the same.

They would say that the spirits of the land watch and judge them, that the spirits of the land watch them every minute of the day and are aware of every thought, deed and action. They're part of the land and beholding to it, so therefore, if you are a speaker of the land, then it will alone make judgment on others. And all they're doing then is acting as mediators between the land and all visitors.

Maybe the land in which they were acting as interlocutors could see what was coming in the future and took pre-emptive action. Maybe it was a bit like, as you told me in Atlantis, as it got closer to the final day the aliens left, but they didn't say anything to anyone and explain why they were leaving. They just left as they sensed or possibly knew that something was amiss and left before the fall and cataclysm.

To begin with I'm not dismissing the credentials or wisdom of any other Elder we've worked with. I believe they're all highly evolved elders, but Karno was different. He just lived a different way. While Kano existed beside a whitefella society, he was never a part of it. He created magic, disappeared, talked to animals, called up eagles and hawks-all things we cannot do today. Was Kano living like the ancient Lemurians of the highest level? Is that the way they lived?.

Mezreth:

If a soul was once Lemurian or Atlantean, they will forever be recognized as such. However, unlike Atlantia, Lemuria is still here and speaks only to those who listen. Atlantean souls have lost their connection to their land but can attain solace through a memory of the clock that can be turned back for the distant future of today. That is why I have hope. There are thousands of Atlanteans to one Lemurian.

Steve:

What he's saying is that Lemuria never vanished under the sea or was wiped out. And by the way, the Original people of Australia say the Dreaming is never finished, it's still here as is the land of Australia, which was part of Lemuria. In that respect the body and soul of Lemuria does still exist.

The Hopi prophecies insist that if you don't learn the Old Teachings, you will not be part of the new world, which is exactly what Mezreth said. And the disappointing outcome of the past indiscretions is that there are thousands of Atlanteans for each

217

Lemurian, that's a bit scary. I think we need a lot more input from the Lemurian side.

(Lea adding commentary):
Well, you got to remember, population wise, Lemuria never really went over a million.

Steve:
I need a bit more clarification and I know Mezreth has answered this, but nonetheless I'll ask anyway. You said earlier that Lemuria was the spiritual wand of the planet of which others were allowed to visit but never stay. Why did others, including Atlanteans need to visit Lemuria?

Mezreth:
Atlantia was a clock, but Atlanteans were deaf to the ticking. The Lemurians could hear it and they saw how deaf Atlanteans were and the Lemurians desperately sympathized.

Steve:
He said that Atlantia was the clock and the Lemurian people had control of the wand. If you have control of the wand, you also have control of the magic it creates.

We have been told that there was a reluctance to sever relations as the Lemurians had obviously had empathy towards the Atlanteans. It can't be that their banishment was due being aggressive towards Lemurians if they've got so much sympathy and concern for them. To an extent they were trying to help through giving them something to think about. Perhaps they were trying to teach them how to hear the clock?

(Lea adding commentary):
They were invited because the Lemurians understood something that the Atlanteans didn't perceive. They were on a timer, essentially.

And the Lemurians were like, we got to help these guys out. And they tried, but alas, failed.

Steve:
It could have been they tried and tried and then realized one day that they just couldn't be helped. It could be they gave it their best shot. It's a bit like today. If you tried that today, you'd have a whole lot of trouble with any group in control listening, just like it was back then.

What spiritual function does Uluru perform in sustaining this Lemurian legacy? Why was Uluru the location where ceremonies were held recently that will transform everything?

Mezreth:
Uluru is the soul of Lemuria. There's the future you now inhabit, and it is where it all began and will all end.

Steve:
Well, it does come back to the soul, it always does. If it's Uluru is the soul of Lemuria, and Lemuria is coming back, then it becomes the soul of the planet, doesn't it? Because if Lemuria is a network as you said before that network spreads all over and of course, that cleansing is still an on-going event. During the second solstice, we asked everyone to give send meditations and their energy towards the red rock. And we're going to do that for the final third ceremony.

And isn't it fascinating that quite recently, Carmen Boulter, who doesn't know or met us, said a major thing was going to happen on exactly the same date the next ceremony will take place. Now, people could say that's a coincidence, but our take the word coincidence is always the easy way out.

I want to talk about the rings of Lemuria simply because they are an accurate reflection of where Lemuria was, and still is. They are of massive diameter. They're not made for normal people or normal fingers.

The question is, the rings are of a massive diameter, were they made for giants and what actually happens when these rings were worn by them?

Mezreth:
Those rings were made for those who embodied Lemuria. They were parted and scattered across the landscapes. Each piece becoming greater than what was before and the Atlanteans realized this.

Steve:
In other words, those rings got stronger.

(Lea adding context):
They fed off of each other. And who was paying attention to them? The Atlanteans. Atlanteans saw that ability and thought it was a good idea to copy.

Steve:
Of course. That's because they're in contact with each other. And they understood that the rings had that power. But as we know, isn't it interesting because the Atlantean rings to begin with had the same power as the Lemurian rings, but they feed off the people who hold them. The same rule for the rocks.

It's exactly the same rule. There are rocks I have that would kill anyone that touched them.

And the only ring I trust, has the three sets of animals (elephant, monkey and pig), because we know it's bound into the land it will never lie to me. It would know not how to mislead and deceive.

(Lea adding context):
Those rings were made for those who embodied Lemuria. Perhaps some or all the ring-bearers happened to be giants, big people.

Steve:

Then it could have been passed on to people of a lower height and stature as long as they were evolved and spiritual. I put it on, and I wear it as often as I can, but I have to be careful because it is so big and wide it will fall off my finger. Of all the deeds, aspirations and intentions of Lemurians, what most impressed Mezreth and why?

Mezreth:

The one thing countless cultures have failed to achieve (and this is countless cultures across the board, not just on humans.) The labyrinth never took the power of faith from the land. Instead, they nurtured it, tended it until it became its own face in turn, the land gave them its land.

Steve:

They become the face of the land. So that's the difference. And, of course, I've made this point often that once a culture starts to fight against nature, there is a heavy price to pay as it must lose everything.

And there's such a difference because there's no nurturing, there's no ceremony. And I'm sure that the Lemurians, like the Original people of Australia, gave ceremony to the land. And that's what we're learning here.

That also that means that we're falling into that Atlantean trap again.

We've been told Aliens did live on Earth in Atlantis for a considerable time. Did the same living arrangements exist on the Lemuria and why did this cease?

Mezreth:

All visitors had to pass through laws and into the belly of Lemuria. The Lemurians, who had been there for countless millennia, were still seen as visitors. Yet their judgment allowed them to stay and learn.

Steve:
Atlantis fell on its sword through its own mistakes and loss of direction. In Lemuria, there were not the same mistakes or loss of direction. So, the question still remains, did other negative circumstances prevail because even if it was spread out in a network, the geographical network disappeared.

Mezreth:
Lemuria is still here and making choices either for the ending or against the ending of the book.

Steve:
Lemuria hasn't lost its direction and integrity because it's still here.

The islands disappeared, and some parts separated. Obviously way back there was a channel that joined Sri Lanka and India to Australia and that went underwater some time ago. The land bridge connecting Australia to New Guinea also disappeared at a different time, possibly around 8,000 years ago. Mainland Australia did get smaller in stages. But when that happened, it wasn't catastrophic, but seemingly quite slow. Like the seas rising, not a tsunami or explosion of power crystals.

(Lea adding commentary):
It took on a different face.

Steve:
Mezreth and the Adnyamathanha (South Australian tribe) said it began here and will end here. I suppose the question isn't so much those two predictions because we've ticked them off. The pivotal phrase stands above scrutiny, for it is our future on offer.

It began here and will end here, and then begin again here. So, what is 'it?'.

(Lea adding commentary:
Yeah. And that was actually something I did want to dissect a little bit more. Lemuria is still making choices either for the ending or against the ending of the Earth book now being written. You got to remember that Lemurians were speakers of the land, and though not by their own choice, they exiled Atlanteans.

Lemuria saw something in Atlanteans that nobody else on the planet could see. But the trick is Lemuria is not a place, it is more a collective of people that saw the clock and saw what was going to happen.

They probably saw what was going to happen to the rest of the world past that point of separation. And it seems like all the choices being made now are for the either for the ending or against the ending of the book of humanity.

Steve:
I think that's exactly right. I wouldn't add much to that because that's what this is all about. Right now, it's about writing the conclusion, the book was opened two years nine months ago, and it closes in another couple of months. It finishes now because it has to.

And then everyone's going to make a decision. But I suppose the decision is, do you want to become as Lemurians did or fall in line with the Atlantean tragedy? The choice is simple, as the Hopi just keep saying the same thing time after time. The Old Teachings always was and always will be the only way forward. And Mezreth has actually said the same thing today.

Transcript Eleven

Steve:

OK, we got a series of questions for Mezreth, and for anyone that does not get this, I just want to quickly explain and recap that Lea is not channelling; she is basically in conversation. There's a huge difference, if she was channelling, most can make up their stories, but in Lea's case, she is not channelling, she is in contact with an alien on the other side of the highest level, or aliens as the case may be, but we won't go into that for now.

Now, I have to be honest, I have a rational mind, I've been to or in school most of my life, and I was a schoolteacher and that does interfere, as I still have moments when I still wonder, whether Lea is either delusional or mad, or a combination of both. Then I read and listen to what Mezreth has to say and the doubts vanish in the haze.

I think that's the best way to judge anything; the same way that we've got Slater's notes that have been slandered and attacked by people that have not read one solitary word that he wrote. Same rules of engagement apply here. The best way to judge whether Lea and I are making this up is to read the results and if the commentary of Mezreth sounds like it came from any human, we could be making this up. But I can tell you now, if it does come from a human, it's not me or Lea making them up, that much is for sure as we are just not that intelligent, insightful or knowledgeable.

And I am hoping I can get some clarity on an unexpected diversion in proceedings and neighbours. That's why the first question I'm asking relates to our visit a week ago when someone or something was in the bush, screaming! Two months ago, I would never even think of raising the topic of yowies, but that changed after what we heard and felt. Evan is a 100% sure, I am 99, 999% sure, because I still have a rational mind that mumbles in the background. Despite the muted protests, it was a yowie making a lot of noise in our forest thirty meters away from where I stood.

Are there actually yowies in our bush, because the scientists still say they do not exist; mind you, the scientists tell us a lot of other things I do not believe. Anyway, if they are wrong, are they from here or off-world in origin?

If they are real, what are their intentions and why are they so wary of adult humans?

Mezreth:
They are the last remaining pure Elementals. They are what you could have been, they are wild but as aware as you. The forests are their cities, and the trees are their skyscrapers, but they see and hear what threatens their homes every single day, and it is not children. Over millennia, they have been forced to adapt to your growing presence; despite their ferocity, they are aware they are not the apex predator of the Earth. That horrid crown is on humans.

Steve:
I did not expect that answer. When Mezreth said 'the last remaining Elementals,' is that the right term? ...

(Lea adding):
Yes sure, Elementals.
Steve:
Elementals? Does that mean they are from here?

(Lea):
Yeah.

Steve:
That's what I thought. Because lot of people are saying they are from somewhere else, like another planet, but I never thought that. The wild forests are their cities and therefore, we are a direct threat to their existence, aren't we? Because, while we chop down their trees, we are destroying their cities? But do we need to fear them?

(Lea adding context):
Before we got the bright idea to control everything, we saw around us, there was a kind of, a peaceful relationship. I mean, when I hear Original Elders speak about yowies, you know, through an indirect information, there is a sense of reverence not, just, respect, a reverence. It's like, we knew they have their areas, they know we have our areas, and we don't interact or interfere and as long as we live in peace then everything will be fine. But that only works as long as respect their boundaries and them. Unfortunately, white fellas didn't care.

Steve:
I have never met an Elder of Old Ways that hasn't raised independently the issue of yowies and little people and has always spoken of them with deep respect. But, it's funny you mentioned that, because my brother, who worked in the Armed Forces, told me stories about troops going out into the bush to camp for the night. Whenever they left the campsite for whatever reason, the yowies would come and trash the place completely and it got to the stage now, where even the Armed Forces won't admit it, there are places where they won't send their people out to camp anymore. No official reason or excuse is given. I have also heard stories that, if you are carrying a gun into the forest, they do regard you as an enemy.

They certainly don't like humans. I didn't mention this before, but will now, I was told once, and it gives you an idea of the real attitude of the yowies, when we were going into their forest/city and the Elders told us that we needed to be careful, and we were given a yowie song to sing before entering. And we were told few things about them, number one, we were to sing a song before we went in there, because they would understand it, and number two if they were to run at us, don't even bother trying to outrun them. It's not going to happen, and don't even bother trying to fight them, because that's not going to happen either. We were told, if they run towards us, find the smallest twig you can and hold it up in the air and wave it at them. When they look at that twig, and then realise straight away, you understand who they are, and that you won't threaten them, and then they will not harm you. We were also told if they run at you very much like a gorilla will, it is like a bluff charge, they do not intend to fight you but to get rid of you.

So, they are the last remaining pure Elementals and when we think about this, we know at the moment there's at least sixteen different hominins that are around our size, but this mob are larger. In the Bible they talk about the fact that there were giants in those days. They even went further than this generalisation in giving one of these "giants' a name, Goliath. Why would that be written unless it's true?

(Lea adding commentary):
And... if I may add a little bit about what you said about putting the stick up as like a sign of 'I'm not a threat' and Yowies read that, and they understand its meaning, doesn't it imply civility?

Steve:
Absolutely. If a lion or crocodile is charging you and you wave a twig, you will still get eaten. Elders always speak of Yowies with the utmost respect and honour of who they are, and like I said, I don't really care what any white fella said, I can't find one black fella that knows the yowie story that doesn't acknowledge the fact that they are there, and most of them have seen them. I've met about four people that have seen them and all of them made it clear, that they honestly believe that yowies have arranged that. It's not as if you come upon them accidentally, they are in control. They make it clear, that they want people to know about them, but they don't want them to get close; and isn't it interesting that no one has ever caught one? And we think we are smarter than them, we are so smart, that we barely can photograph them, and although we had that chance, we didn't embrace that opportunity.

Everyone was criticising Evan, demanding to know why he didn't tape the screaming. But they weren't there in the pitch black metres from the forest, being overwhelmed by waves of fear., We should follow extend the reach and height of this topic because if I talk about yowies and I don't mention the little people, then Donny and Allen, and all the other black fellas who gave us advice are going to that say we didn't do this properly, that you have to talk about their cousins, the little people And we will. The second question relates to something the covers two important aspects of the little Original people of Australia.

We took Harries Carrol, who is featured on the TV show Bondi Rescue, into country at Kariong. His six-year-old son, Billy, came with him. Billy saw a little hairy man watching him, he told his father that he could see a little yowie, and he did. All Original keepers of Old Lore believe they exist also. And they are right, and if so, what are their skills and talents and why is it they are so drawn to play with, and even kidnap for a time, human children? There are actually stories about them taking children for two or three days and then putting them back. So, what can he tell us about these little ones? Are they the same group as the yowies or different?

Mezreth:
Those beings are as clever as adults, but their hearts are as children. If you are gifted to their frequency, they will welcome you if they are confident in your intent. Like their larger and more potent cousins, the little men are also aware of the viciousness of grown men. However, the little men know this wasn't always so. They aspire to bond with fledgelings, in the hopes they can subdue this terrifying aspect of men.

Steve:
So, they are cousins. In a way. When Billy saw them, he told his dad, he said: 'Daddy, there's a little yowie hiding there,' It was only about two feet tall. We had spoken about the little people earlier in the day, I showed him photographs of ones that looked exactly like us, and the hairy ones don't. They are as clever as us, but they have the hearts of children. That's a good thing, isn't that what most humans

really want? I do know Picasso was obsessed about being able to paint like a child.

(Lea adding commentary): It would be nice to get that back, and I guess in a way, with interacting with kids and bonding with kids they are trying to re-seed that.

Steve:
And if you ask the Elders, and they'll tell you the same thing, the little people love the children, but they are very wary of us. Clearly, they are part of that same group because they have a lot of hair all over their body like the bigger mob, so I suppose that's why Mezreth called them cousins. That means they got some sort of relationship with each other; if you go back far enough, there's got to be a common genetic ancestry for both of them. For them to evolve so dramatically in height and other ways, but that's going back a long way.

(Lea adding commentary):
Yea, we don't know, I mean, Mezreth did not specify who that was, where they were, that information… maybe if you ask, I suppose for next time…

Steve:
We'll do that on another occasion. And that probably explains also why they, the little people are always called the masters of camouflage. You could walk past them, and you wouldn't see them. And with the yowies, well, they seem to be masters of disappearing and turning up if and when they want. So, they do have that in common. I did not know they were cousins, but I knew they had a relationship of some form.

With the big and little hairy Original people discussed, albeit ever so briefly, I did want to ask Mezreth some questions about Frederic Slater and the written interpretations he left behind. The reason being his records of Original engravings could be the most important notes written by an archaeologist anywhere at any particular time, ever. Because he says that within these pages are the keys to understand all of the stone age engravings and this is what's really fascinating, he claims that stone age engravings which he calls pictograms, are an international phenomenon. So, what he is saying, is that all of the people of the ancient past were far more civilized than the people and societies of today. One part of his opening commentary claims that when humans came here, they were fully evolved with seven senses, more empathetic and aware than we are today. We were at our pinnacle then and we've been falling backwards ever since. This is open contradiction with the experts who claim we were far more primitive and duller, and slowly evolved to where we are now, the pinnacle of progress. Who was right, and if it is Slater, why does he use the term "we came here'?"

Mezreth:
You were never fully evolved, but you are not entirely made by the hands of nature.

Steve:
Ok, we were never fully evolved, but this came about not just through the hands of nature, which we knew. It is a combination of what was brought here, which was the template, and then moulded "by the hands of nature." It seems that we began at a position that was promising, and now we've regressed to a stage which is abysmal.

Let's get back to the stage we are at now, the mess we are trying to fix things up. There's a particular moment in time, the global change taking place that is full of hope and redemption, but I heard something Mezreth said last time that made me a little worried. He said that for every Lemurian soul incarnate right now, there are thousands of Atlantean souls present and on world. Knowing that the oncoming changes heavily relies upon Lemurian wisdom and aspirations, isn't the sheer bulk of those with Atlantean leanings and potential failings too much of a hurdle to overcome in these times?

My thinking is, if it is well over a thousand to one, it would sound like the odds aren't great to orchestrate the change when you've got such a massive percentage of people that have no empathy or familiarity with the presence of Lemuria, so how do we get around that one?

Mezreth:
You know now, why it failed before. History does not have to repeat itself. The east and west are not superior over the other; if either one overcomes the other, another failure will be your future. What we hope for is seeing the marriage of east and west, both must compromise for the sake of each other.

Steve:
Isn't it interesting how he refers to Atlantis and Lemuria as east and west? So, to an extent, what we are talking about, is the western lifestyle, which is trying to dominate the world, which is all about consumerism, becoming an economic statistic and making money no matter what happens. In the opposite side of the circle, you've got an eastern culture which is more religious, and more in contact with the concept of reincarnation and some form of karma or spirits watching every word and deed.

While we are speaking about that change, I wanted to change sources and go completely left field by quoting from a song by 'Yes', which was written and sung by John Anderson. There are two lines I feel are very relevant, "We began at the first spring, that the promise will come when the promise is made." Now, I've always have found those two lines fascinating. What is the promise, and can you describe what that first spring is?

Mezreth:
The promise is the answer to the question of why you came here at this time. To see spring, you must endure the winter; you have never seen spring, you came close once before, and maybe you will see it this time.

Steve:

I honestly believed that's actually why we are meant to be on this planet, I believe it is all about that one question. So, we've had to make that promise. The whole point of our existence is to work out why. So, John Anderson was right! I think there was one word in his last answer I want to confirm first, Lea could you read those last two sentences again, I think there is one word I'd like to focus on a bit more.

Mezreth: (via Lea)

To see spring, you must endure the winter. You have never seen spring, you came close once before, and maybe you will see it again this time.

Steve:

The word 'maybe,' that is a seminal equivocation. We are supposed to rediscover that spring again, and I'm pretty sure, when he is talking about that past, he is talking about Atlantis and Lemuria, I've got no doubt.

There is a possibility for each person that change will come again. I noticed he didn't call it 'a definite,' he called it a "maybe', didn't he? And we can still screw up.

Remaining focussed on this spring the next question relates to making sure this spring is sung up. That is all about Uluru. For a lot of good reasons, and one is that's where the ceremony took place, and it is the spiritual soul of the planet. If, as you said earlier, Uluru is the spiritual soul of what was Lemuria, which was a spiritual wand, this location must be so sacred and powerful. Because of all these blessings this is an important question, how can individuals make personal contact with Uluru? If it is Mother Earth's spiritual soul, it would really be important for every person on this planet to have the chance to connect. How can people get closer to the spring?

Mezreth:

It doesn't matter how far you are, Uluru can hear your song and Lemuria will always respond, Lemuria always responds.

Steve:

He keeps talking about Lemuria as being not in the past tense, doesn't he? And he always talks about Atlantis in the past tense. Which means Lemuria never disappeared. Which is what Australia represents doesn't it? This is what this is about.

And we know it's still here because, unfortunately, you did not get that experience, but I did, I had the fortunate experience of meeting and talking to an Original Elder living like a Lemurian would, by the name of Karno. I do know there are other Original people, not many, I'd be counting them on two hands, that are still living that way. I know one around our way, there's a gentleman around here, called Uncle Lewis Walker and we had him on our on-line conferences, twice. He sees things just like Karno. This is why Mezreth keeps telling us, Lemuria never went away.

(Lea adding commentary): Well, I mean, it's only if you throw that line out it responds.

Steve:

In some ways it is that simple, you just have to throw a line out do it with good intentions, will it reach the soul of this planet. By throwing a line out to Uluru, I don't think there's really a technique to that; it's just a matter of you saying to yourself 'I want to commit to that rock, and I want to feed from that rock. I want to learn from that rock, I want to be a part of it. That's how to throw a line out.

(Lea adding context):

It's the equivalent of touching the wand. You can only channel if you are actually connected to the wand.

Steve:

We are in the wand, but unfortunately, you have to find out which way the wand's pointing, which is Uluru, and then earn the right to hold it. So, he looks upon the story about the destruction of Atlantis and Lemuria as being half right, and half wrong. The other point people must remember, and Lea can testify to this, is that Atlantis literally and figuratively blew itself up.

I am sure that the shock waves that went throughout the planet, because even archaeologists will admit to this event, but do so grudgingly, that at around 12,000 years ago 95% of world population disappeared.

And then they'll say 'ahh, it was due to a... oh... it wasn't a meteor, we did have one 65 million years ago; no, it couldn't be that it's due to, oh, a sudden Ice Age, and I'm thinking...

There have been eight Ice Ages before, and we got them. We got through every one of them. And there was an Ice Age taking place in Europe 750,000 years ago, and the climate and resource base changed dramatically; from one type of lifestyle to another. The Denisovans and Neanderthals coped and adapted to without any apparent hardship in those new areas; they rearranged their lifestyle and went with the change in climate and flora and fauna.

As to the geographical demise of the Lemurian confederation With Lemuria, my understanding is that a lot of the land just went under the waters, and the Pacific Islands are the bits that stick up, like peaks on the top of the sunken lands below. Lemuria didn't disappear completely because Australia still stands, and of course, the Easter Island remains as does Hawaii all those bits and pieces that are still with us.

Still on the same topic, but with a difference in that the content behind this question is not ours but belongs to Sarah. This comes from one of the people that has been working with us recently and has been very helpful too. Normally when people tell me a vision, I say that's great, it could be true, as I don't know. But I am going to take this a bit further, because Sarah had some visions that go back to the first ceremony at Uluru.

While at Uluru, Sarah had a vision that while the UFO hovered over Uluru during the ceremony, and for anyone that is not sure about her authenticity or they think such talk is nonsense, go to our web site; there is an article where we filmed it. And honestly, once you see the film of Uluru exploding into sheet of intense blanketing the sky and another video of what could only be a UFO slowly flying above the rock at the same time, you won't so readily question Sarah's honesty or sanity. This is what she said; she sensed and saw a powerful feminine energy or entity leave the ship and merge into the big red rock. That was a bit of a shock then but certainly has visual backing. My question for Mezreth is what is it that actually happened, what did the lens see when the white light burst forth from the red rock?

Mezreth:
Humans are not the only ones that have hummed to Uluru. We bond with you in many ways; not just with speakers. We want you to see the universe from where we are.

Steve:
I didn't expect that, I was hoping for something about light. But he does refer to seeing the universe, was that flash of white light the essence of the Universe? Were we getting dowsed in God particles when the light exploded out of Uluru? And it's clear in the footage, when the sheet of white surges out, it covers the entire horizon but does not infinitesimally mix, lighten or fade the colour and edges of the red rock. Which is really enticing and validating as that clear colour delineation between the sky on top and rock below goes a long way towards conclusively proving that Uluru exploded in universal white light at 7:36 pm, December 21, 2020. This so much more than fascinating and most assuredly confirming, because it increases the importance of that strange massive red rock in the middle of nowhere, that doesn't seem to belong. it really does sort of increase the importance of that enigmatic rock in red. They had to have an involvement, especially since Mezreth spoke of bonding in many ways, and clearly one of those means of communication was the use of Uluru being "speakers" or amplifiers of this process of bonding us to them. Sounds like a real good idea. Where do I sign up?

(Lea adding commentary):
And it… and it seems like that there is an implication that they're connecting through Uluru to us.

Steve:
Absolutely, if as the Bible declares that sound came first, then if using the speakers which transmit that sound, why not pick the soul of the planet to amplify this sacred playlist? Which means it's a bit like, if you want to get on to that rocky royal telephone, you have to start by ringing up Uluru. That is the obligatory first step, otherwise you are not going get any further down the line. We do know that the feminine aspect of the planet has now exploded, filmed and testified to. There is something every Elder I've spoken to has said about the past and future. What is quite it's interesting is that their observations never vary about two things. When I have spoken about the on-coming change in every circumstance, they always reply that it will be feminine. It's no different when the subject of Black-fella magic is raised, whenever I ask about which gender of magic has got the stronger power, there is only one reply, women. But when you look at that, you sort of feel all the men in this incarnation, are really starting this show at a disadvantage.

(Lea adding commentary):
This bond and the compromise of the East and West Mezreth speaks of could be symbolic. We believe Mezreth was talking of a historical setting involving Atlantis and Lemuria.

Steve:
Let's stay down this track a bit, because as we get closer to the change that's ahead, I'm going to be re-stating questions asked earlier, but I'll add something to it. In that semi-repetitive vain I partially asked this before, but not specifically in these words. Is the Earth the only planet that's heartbeat vibration, which is measured through the Shuman resonance, is increasing so rapidly?

Mezreth:
No, far from the only one.

Steve:
So, a lot of planets are ascending in this time now?

(Lea adding context):
I would say changing. I mean, Mezreth is very careful when it comes to when he uses the word and meaning of ascension. He is always very careful when he uses the word change; change can imply for the better, maybe ascension, or it can be for the worse. I really hope we don't fall backwards, and for the sake of those other worlds, I don't want that to happen either, because that sounds awful.

Steve:
Is this something that's happening in other places as it is here too at the same time?

(Lea adding commentary):
Yeah, roughly at the same time.

Steve:
That does lead on to a question about whether that's by design or by accident; but I'll ask that another time. We get reports all the time, from people about the Shuman resonance and how often it is accelerating to readings never seen or sensed before. Whereas before it would shoot up every now and then, every couple of months there'll be a little peak; now it's nearly a daily or weekly event where it's really just ramping up constantly. And I'm wondering what is the immediate impact of the huge increase, I'm not talking about down the line and what it leads up to, what is the immediate impact this has on human beings living on this planet now? Is it positive, negative or both?

Mezreth:

The turmoil is akin to what happened before, but to see spring, you need to understand how to overcome it forever. This is the best way for each individual to have this foundation laid. Without this, you will lack the wisdom for future challenges.

Steve:

So, that is a yes, it's like the turmoil from before, but there's been so much turmoil here and on so many occasions and it would be hard to determine which ones were there before, just all of them would be the best way to look at that. Is there an implication there that if we do this correctly, it has eternal consequences here?

(Lea adding commentary):

He is not going to be black and white specific, he never completely implied the opposite, that if we manage to overcome this set of challenges or trials, then we will never have to repeat them again. This respite is real, but temporary. It doesn't mean that we are free from all challenges and trials for the rest of eternity; he doesn't say that it's like that. No there will be more, but you going to have to get this level finished, sorted, done and dusted, before you get to that next point, but if you keep avoiding it, it will still keep ascending. The challenges are there forever, it will keep coming up until…

Steve:

In other words, I think it runs like this: if there were no challenges and drama in the future, there wouldn't be much point in reincarnating here.

(Lea adding commentary):
There is no life.

Steve:

There is no no point. Because if there is no challenge, there's nothing to test your metal, to find out what and who you really are. Because

238

for some people, and we won't get too personal about this, it could be appalling, life after life after life, but that will be a consequence of their choices. But in every situation, they still have the potential to improve themselves, and that's what this is all about.

I suppose what that means is the mundane stupid things we do at the moment, we might ignore them, but there will be other challenges but more subtle and this time the consequences will not spread further so the collateral damage will be restricted to the perpetrator. But, at the moment, we are basically still in the kindergarten class squabbling in the sand pit, that's about as far as we've have reached. If we get pass this before the third solstice which will be the line in the sand, we can move on to struggles, issues and misunderstandings.

Central to this ascension is absorbing the breadth and implications of the word 'evil,' particularly after listening to Mezreth's description of what good and evil is. He seems to be saying that everything is on the same line, and it is all about degrees of intention. In one of our rock workshops I read out a report in a book where an Elder, who was offended by someone when they did something wrong and they and deserved to be punished by being speared through the leg. But if he made a mistake and killed that person he'd be killed also. Mezreth would argue that's wrong. He would claim that this is all about your intentions, never the result.

(Lea adding context):
No, Mezreth does not have favourites, except if you are a reject, a rebel or basically just the stuff you find under the bins, he likes only those types.

Steve:
So that is why he takes an interest in us, but let's not get personal here… we are supposed to keep some of our private indiscretions at elbow's length, and let's keep them like that. Moving on to the next question and this one is a little bit longer, in fact, it is one of my longest questions asked. I do respect people who are psychologists and psychiatrists whose main role is to help people who cannot cope,

which is very noble, but I feel that the way they try to cure people actually creates more problems than it solves. I don't think they fully understand why people came to this life with baggage and insecurities.

Each incarnation is an opportunity for each human to find their inner balance, connection with nature and Old Way teaching and philosophy, and equally, resolve past-life issues and mistakes. And also, come with grips with their inner faults and demons. If so, and we are basically a product of our past incarnations, how do we resolve these long-term failings now? Most psychiatrists and psychologists do not even accept this notion and explanation but would suggest therapies and drugs will assist; so how can humans treat problems that are deliberately hidden from each soul and most therapists whenever they incarnate on this planet? So, my problem is this: I came here with a lot of past-life baggage and most of it is not very good. Now, I could have gone to a psychologist or psychiatrist, and I would say that most of the suggestions given to me would be actually counterproductive.

My question is this: If we are going heal ourselves, how are we going do this, because if we go to a psychologist or psychiatrist, they will give us drugs or therapy that will not address the fact that most of the things we are doing today are the product of what we did before. So, how do humans clean themselves up in these final moments and get themselves organised, when the mainstream answer to cleanse yourself will actually make the problem worse. So, that solution becomes the problem for humans during these turbulent times, where many people are starting to sense the good and bad within them; in some cases, more bad than good, but how do they fix themselves?

Mezreth:
This is a test for all times and all manner of beings, not just humans but beings. This fine balance is something we have all walked and we continue to walk for the sake of our continual evolutions. There will never be a time of true serenity in life; life itself is chaos by default. What the point is, is to find an everlasting and beneficial chaos. This

is also traumatic for a soul and in turn, trauma for the body. Find your sense and then you will find your purpose. The challenge is realising your reality, your purpose will never match another's. So, to impose one's reality and compare one's to another inhibits the soul, the person's ability to find purpose to find self. The inner universe is the only thing that exists. All beyond is a mere reflection.

Steve:

There is a bit in there. I love the last part, 'the inner universe is the only reality that exists'. What he is saying indirectly is the outer universe, which is the sun, the moon, the planets and the constellations, is merely the stage. And I also like the fact that this life is chaos by default, that's a stunning observation! So, it's one big Cosmic test, isn't it? And what he is saying very simply is that comparing ourself to others, will achieve nothing. And essentially that's what psychiatry and psychology provide the person under stress.

We have new days and ways looming up on the horizon and we need to reach the minimum pass mark. The reality is, living on this side does come down to you finding peace and purpose with your own internal comparisons, and don't use it against anyone else. Because if you do that, if you compare yourself to other people, you'll never win and you'll always lose. When you start comparing yourself with someone else that is an acknowledgement that you feel like you need something that's not there, that you are failing in some respect whenever you compare yourself to someone who you mistakenly think isn't failing.

What you don't realise is that those people are failing in other respects and when they compare themselves, they get trapped in the same circles of inadequacies. It really doesn't matter who the comparison is made to, whoever it is they have their own demons and flaws. Mahatma Gandhi is understandably revered by many, I have read at least a dozen books about him, watched a few films documenting his life and many great deeds and insights. I used to think at one stage, that there's an example of someone who is on such a high level that I'll never reach. That changed when I found out he was not perfect; he often treated his wife and family very badly, and two of his children were so messed up inside they committed suicide.

(Lea adding commentary):
I didn't know that.

Steve:
They hated their lives so much that they saw no reason to live. Then you take another person I still admire called Albert Einstein. He made his wife walk three steps behind him; and most of the greatest discoveries he made, were made either in conjunction with his wife, or she was mainly responsible. But, when you start looking very carefully, if you start looking at all these so-called great people, you will find the faults never go away. It is so dangerous trying to compare yourself against anyone which is what psychiatrists do, they tell you what your normal is when they still haven't found themselves.

(Lea adding commentary):
You won't find it. In a way it leaks back to the whole concept of chaos. What we consider to be order and chaos is a completely and utterly relative concept. Your life may seem to be chaotic and if you were to compare it to another person's life you know, they may appear orderly and content, but beneath the surface in the deep recesses, there will be secrets and unresolved desires.

Steve:
Definitely right and that desire for familiarity and comfort reminds me of something that at face value is very clever politics. There was a politician in Australia called John Howard and when he got into power and led the country, he did so by waxing lyrically about the fifties and early sixties, about a time when there was law and order. And that stability was everything, there was less crime, plenty of obedience and people towed the line. But the order he pined for had a heavy price to pay. The wife would stay home, make the meals, wash

the dishes and clean up and when the husband would come home late in the afternoon, she would put on his slippers, then make his food, and then he might go to the pub for a while with his mates and get drunk. Then maybe come home and bash her a bit, and that was considered order! Because everyone did the same thing.

(Lea):
It was normal?

Steve:
This was all a normal part of day-to-day life, and everyone was normal, there was no chaos, everyone was the same. John Howard and others waxed lyrically about this time when everything was predictable, it was predictably boring, it was predictably unchallenging, and it was predictably insular. At that time the law said we didn't have black fellas, in the national census Original people were not counted as humans but given the same status as an animal like the kangaroo, their normality was being a third-class citizen.

I am inclined to think that the most vibrant times were the late sixties and early seventies when the young people of the world saw that same order as stifling, numbing and repressive. There was a line in a song by the Who, 'I hope I die before I get old' which was an anthem and came about because they despised the comparisons made by the older people.

So, what then happened was they rebelled, they started taking drugs, women became slightly more promiscuous because they wanted to be, and that was their right. People started to do radical things, they challenged fundamental norms that underpinned a very conservative global society. I remember walking down the streets with long hair and people would throw things and insult me. They did so justified by their fact, I was disorderly. The hippie generation grew out of that repudiation of a society that denied freedom of choice. I believe that decade of unfettered protest and innovative thinking was the best ten years that ever existed on this planet.

And then, we had punk and disco music, and all mainstream media and politicians went about vilifying and ridiculing anyone who dared to look elsewhere, and then people started to fall back in line. And I feel like right now we've gone back to the early sixties again, where people are now questioning everything and saying 'I don't believe this anymore, I think that's wrong. I think that can be a dangerous thing because it leads to stagnation, apathy and to fitting into the mainstream norm. I've learned one thing about the mainstream norm, it's more often than not based on a lie. So, yes I agree with Mezreth I love the chaos by default, I think that's a perfect description of what's taking place, but I agree too, that chaos under the right conditions only comes out of an ordered society that's become stagnant, is imploding and has no moral compass. I mean, honestly, what intelligent thoughts and actions came out of the fifties?

So, I embrace the chaos, I think it's a great idea, because out of chaos comes change. And the change is coming, real soon. As the Schuman residence keeps ramping up this change, will that see the so-called junk DNA and the brain running at 15% capacity both spark up if the soul is willing and committed? But what happens to those amongst us who are not ready for this redemptive chaos?

Mezreth:
The ones who go on will be changed for the better as one may imagine but there will come a worse time, remember the cost of arrogance! Humility is the lantern in the dark. Yes, you are open to vulnerability, but you will be seen as true and trusted. Knowing and embracing your strengths and weaknesses may bring you higher. But you asked what happens to those without lanterns: they remain untouched, unseen, and blind in the dark. The cruellest karma that can befall a soul is nothing; they don't' grow, they don't change, they linger in life, but they are already dead.

Steve:
Well, that's good news for one group, for the other group that's a bit worse than I thought. I thought there would be some sort of... I

don't know… some sort of incentive, or something waving in the distance that might cushion the pain and disarray. So even with this change that is taking place, it's not written in cement or rock, but within your soul.

(Lea adding commentary):
The problem he says is, 'if you start believing you are better, you've already lost'.

Steve:
He did say that you got to learn to hate yourself, in doing that you keep your humility, and you don't let you get it in front of yourself. It maybe that is the first step to be taken, because you are not perfect. If you were you would be sitting alongside Mezreth offering advice.

I think that would be a lost cause, of which none of us are entitled, that would be like giving advice to Karno, when it comes to Original culture. I would say nothing and just shut up, I wouldn't say a word. You got to know when to hold your tongue and allow your ears a free rein. I've dealt with quite few people, and I know you have too Lea, that claim that they are in the fast-flowing river the Hopi speak of, that they are fully evolved and understand everything.

From my perspective that sounds very much like the concern that Mezreth has about the future, if the people started talking like that nothing good will come out of it, it would then implode upon itself. So, this change that began at Uluru a couple of years ago when the Earth is going to ascend is going to happen, he's admitted that. However, the fate and destiny of each human is still an unknown package. Even the ones who actually do stay, still have to retain the potential to fall into the same ignorant and arrogant mind-set that caused others to lead to you into believing "you are better." Nothing has been written in stone.

(Lea):
No.

Steve:
So, the earth is ascending, right? We are given an opportunity to ascend. But when we do that, we better make sure that one part doesn't ascend and lead the way, which is our ego.

(Lea adding commentary):
Well, it's... think of it this way, the Earth will always be changing, it will always be growing, it will always be metamorphosizing, but it's up to us to object or go along with it. If we fall behind, we will fall away from here for a long time. The earth won't stop and wait for us, it would be like: 'Are you guys coming?' It won't wait, it doesn't, it won't stop, it does not care, it will keep going forward. But we are the ones who suffer the consequences if we decide to linger behind and to squabble over whatever the situation or challenge is facing us at that point in time. And this includes the 'better time' that is coming. Just because it's an improved time, doesn't mean it is liberated of all the nonsense. I mean a great example, Atlanteans, they hit a point in society that is by all accounts so much higher and evolved, it was so much greater, but...

Steve:
It still failed.

(Lea adding context):
It still failed, they believed their own bullshit, they fell ... what killed them was, they fell in love with their legend.

Steve:
That's of course, that's the issue with the rings; they are part of that fault, that they did fall in love with themselves and to an extent; what I am saying about those people who are claiming they are in the river, I would ask them this, if Mezreth really admires humility, are you being humble or boastful in claiming that you have reached perfection?

(Lea adding commentary):
They never have, never will. I don't know, and I don't care I'm doing my thing.

Steve:
I mean, I used to think that I had a 50% chance of evolving, but I after hearing some information recently I brought it back down to 5%. I think it's a really healthy thing to do and I think it's really important to make that point, he said that we were in this spring once before during the times of Atlantis and we screwed it up. So, what he is saying okay we are going put some of you back in that spring again, but remember, you were there before …

(Lea):
And look what happened.

Steve:
Well, like you said, you were mundane and everyone else was psychic and telepathic, you may think that once you had those paranormal skills you would have become an evolved being. But I've learned through talking to Mezreth and yourself about what has happened before, it does not work like that. There are people that are far more advanced on a psychic and paranormal level, that are not evolved at all, and they don't care about other aspects. There's that one small eternal issue, your ego, if it takes over. The soul can't be blinded by its own magnificence.

(Lea adding commentary):
Mezreth says: 'Humility is a lantern in the dark,' We are all open to vulnerability because you are exposing yourself essentially to existential threats. Your defence must be to know and embrace your strengths and weaknesses. But what happens to those without a lantern, the ones without humility? They remain, untouched, they are unseen, and they are blind to the dark, and the worst thing that can happen to them is nothing. Nothing happens.

Steve:

Do you know what that sounds like to me, it sounds exactly the same as the most feared punishment in Original society, which is you are banished, and you can't come back to country, and they say your soul is lost forever and it can never grow. It sounds like a nearly identical description of a soul that has been banished from its tribal lands. And to a large extent what's happening here and now is, if you don't stay you will be banished from your tribal planet. There is no difference in anything bar the scope of geography, it's the same story.

A recurring question I never leave alone, and others do ask me this, is what happens to those who the planet rejects? I know it is primarily bad news, but I've always been of the opinion that there is a way out for them. I have this idea, and it is not something given to me, that they go and incarnate on another planet and maybe get better and come back, but …

(Lea adding commentary):

I don't think he is talking about necessarily what takes place after, he talks about the journey. And remember this event is universal and he is not just focussing on humans here, this is about what happens across the cosmos, and effects all beings.

Steve:

It's a general statement.

(Lea adding commentary):

Yes, it definitely is a general statement.

Steve:

So we are not the only group that is going through this upheaval and chaos, with a change ahead, it's happening all over.

(Lea adding commentary):
Under these on-coming changes in circumstance Mezreth did say that 'the cruellest karma that can befall the soul is nothing'. It is the death of a 'thousand cuts' but without pleasure or pain. Just think about that for a second. That actually terrifies me, the idea that there is no possibility of ... if you are not met with some semblance of stimulus, like no new thing, nothing at all. You are stuck in a cage, you are stuck in rut, you are imprisoned in yourself where 'they linger in life, but they are already dead'.

Now, he is not necessarily implying that they are physically alive, or that they are literally dead, it's just a complete lack of soul purpose. When you are alive, you are incarnated because there is a purpose to it. If you don't have that, you don't have anything and you are nothing.

Steve:
Which is the exactly the punishment the Original people would give someone who broke a fundamental sacred law, their life would be spared but their soul would suffer for an eternity in being banished from their land and tribe, forever. For this to happen, the crime would not be theft or murder, it would have to be a spiritual transgression of the highest order. For that sort of punishment to be that severe, I don't think it would be handed out...

(Lea):
Willingly?

Steve:
No, this would have to be for the most despicable sacred crimes that are unforgivable. To a large extent that's what we are talking about right now. That's why that analogy is so strong, because the outcome of what we are talking about now is exactly the same outcome that Original people were talking about then. Your soul could be suspended within as a type of personal limbo.

I know that more than once I have asked Mezreth for some advice that could assist in understanding and preparing for the change, and he did reply but while the answers were undoubtedly correct, they were somewhat short and cryptic. It wasn't as if he set out a guide with ten easy steps as such.

However, if all of his answers, suggestions and warnings were put into one resource or publication, which in this case is this book, we believe such a compilation would be invaluable and certainly set people on the right track. That is the main reason why this book was put together. There is an off-world rule regarding contact, it cannot include landing a UFO on the White House lawn and taking over the running of everything, or handing out a manifesto that everyone must follow, this cannot be a repeat of Chairman Mao's little red book. So, this is their guidance and recommendations via someone incarnated on this planet in human form, which in this case is Lea. You can dismiss this as being a concocted set of lies, or a delusional woman who has lost all touch with reality, or then again, it could be true. The choice is yours as it always has been. Truth or fiction, you decide.

Sitting for your Final Exam
Steve Strong

You now have some of Mezreth's content and all the syllabus needed, clearly set out and explained. Now comes the final step before the Event overwhelms and cleanses the planet. But there is one seminal equivocation leading up to the Event. The rule is that every incarnated soul presently residing on this planet has to earn a pass and rite of passage. For humans, unlike all other life on this planet who never broke any of Nature's Laws, the privilege to remain is not guaranteed anymore, but it is negotiable.

Everything depends on whether you obey the Hopi obligatory requirement of understanding and absorbing what they call 'Old Teachings.' To that end, there are three interrelated areas of content in this admission test in which nothing less than a pass in each subject is satisfactory. All of this, from our inception onwards to these final days has always been about what, why and who.

What is magic, what obligations do we have to Nature and what is love?

Why are there bad people, why did Aliens come here and why do we die?

Who am I, who are the many different types of Alien beings and who created me?

Mezreth has given you all the answers. But that's only half the task at hand, as knowing the answer is not the same as being the answer.

CPSIA information can be obtained
at www.ICGtesting.com
Printed in the USA
BVRC090829180423
662562BV00004B/62

*9 7 8 0 6 4 8 6 7 7 3 2 1 *